nosh
for STUDENTS

a fun student cookbook

JOY MAY

Other books by Joy

NEW! 30% MORE RECIPES THAN PREVIOUS EDITION

vegetarian nosh
for **STUDENTS**
a fun student cookbook

OVER **100,000** STUDENT NOSH BOOKS SOLD   **Joy May**

ISBN:9780954317973

101 QUESTIONS
**STUDENTS ASK
ABOUT COOKING**

From the author of bestselling student cookbook "Nosh 4 Students"

Written & illustrated by **Joy May**

ISBN:9780954317966

nosh
for **GRADUATES**

Joy May

ISBN:9780954317959

NOSH
BOOKS.COM

Contents

Introduction

This book which was originally inspired by Ben, my oldest son, as he left for uni with virtually no cooking skills. His staple of toasted sandwiches, milk and Mars Bars weren't enough to sustain him. He needed to be able to cook. I started by sending him recipe cards, but without photos, it just didn't inspire him to get the pots and pans out to cook. I looked for good student recipe books, but, at the time, there were none with photos and Ben wanted to see what he was aiming at. I realised something more proactive was in order, so I started to write the first edition of what became "Nosh4Students".

Since first publishing the book back in 2002, we have been helping people, like Ben, to cook for themselves and, hopefully, get beyond just surviving into actually enjoying to cook.

Simple Key

How much it will cost per person.

How easy it is to make. 1 star being super-easy and 5 stars more adventurous.

How many people the recipe will feed.

How long it will take to prepare the meal.

How long it takes to cook the food (oven or hob).

How long you might have to leave the food to cool in the fridge or freezer.

Either it is vegetarian, or has a vegetarian option.

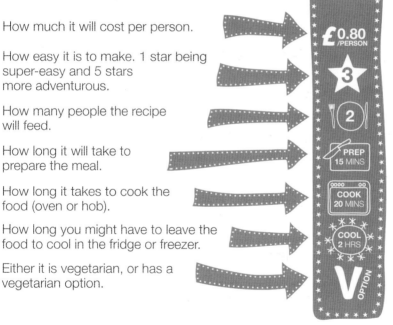

£0.80 /PERSON

3

2

PREP 15 MINS

COOK 20 MINS

COOL 2 HRS

V OPTION

Recipe costs

The recipe costs in this book are an average between Tesco's and Sainsbury's and are the prices at the time of writing. To keep the pricing very relevant, we will update them each time we do a new print run.

One of the key features of this book is that you do not need weighing scales and special measuring equipment. These things are scarcely found in student accommodation.

Throughout the book I have used a mug to measure ingredients. This mug holds ½ a pint of liquid and is the size of the mug pictured opposite.

a mug =

ACTUAL SIZE

All you need

- ☑ mug (approx ½ pint)
- ☑ tablespoon, size mum serves with
- ☑ dessertspoon, one you eat cereal with
- ☑ teaspoon, one you stir tea with
- ☑ wooden spoon
- ☑ chopping board
- ☑ sharp knife
- ☑ small pan with lid
- ☑ medium sized pan, with lid
- ☑ slotted turner (fish slice)
- ☑ frying pan
- ☑ wok
- ☑ casserole dish, with lid
- ☑ colander
- ☑ flat roasting dish, or metal non-stick cooking tray
- ☑ cheese grater
- ☑ mixing bowl
- ☑ cake tin
- ☑ loaf tin

Good buying ideas

It is good to **plan a menu for the week.** This makes cooking much easier, since you will not be dashing to the shops the whole time for little things. It also means you will not waste food, as you will just buy what you need for the week. Try the planner on the opposite page.

Buy in 'bulk' when things are on offer in the supermarkets. Separate into portions in airtight freezer bags and store in your freezer drawer.

Buy whole chickens and cook them. Use the meat for one meal, then use the rest later for sandwiches, baked potatoes, salads, or risottos. This is much cheaper than buying ready-cooked chicken and it is a whole lot tastier.

Always make sure, that **when you visit home**, you return to uni having 'creamed off' any excess from mum's cupboards!

If your parents, or anyone you know, **shop at wholesalers** such as Costco or Makro, get them to buy stuff in bulk for you. Bring it to uni in smaller portions. You'll save a fortune in the long run.

I'm a RENEWAB
natural fibres s
environment - a

weekly Food planner

This menu should cost approximately **£16-18 for the week.**

This plan assumes that you will eat sandwiches and fruit for lunch each day and cereal or toast for breakfast.

Shopping List

- bread
- cereal
- spread/butter
- sandwich fillings (ham, pâtés, cheese, eggs)
- fruit for lunches
- milk
- 1.5 kg chicken
- 4 large potatoes
- 2 onions
- tin condensed mushroom soup
- tin tuna
- 500g Cheddar cheese
- 1 packet of plain crisps
- 250g pack of minced beef
- 400g tin tomatoes
- 400g tin baked beans

Menu

Sunday Roast Chicken p88

Monday eat rest of chicken (you could make it into a salad)

Tuesday Tuna Bake p39

Wednesday eat rest of Tuna Bake

Thursday Jacket Potatoes with Cheese p20

Friday Chilli Con Carne p74

Saturday Eat rest of Chilli

check cupboards for:

- cooking oil
- pasta
- garlic
- stock cubes
- chilli powder

For more weekly food plans see p 200-203

Storecupboard and Fridge

Here are some basics to keep in your storecupboard and fridge. In student halls, or shared houses, you will usually have a shelf in the fridge, one drawer in the freezer and a cupboard to yourself.

FRIDGE/FREEZER

spare loaf of bread in freezer
spare pint of milk in freezer
(plastic not glass bottles)
butter/spread
milk
eggs
cheese
mayo
curry paste

STORECUPBOARD

rice
pasta
cereal
tin chopped tomatoes
tin baked beans
Worcestershire sauce
pilau rice seasoning (livens up rice)
soy sauce
oil to cook with
salt and pepper
stock cubes

tea
coffee
sugar
flour

Useful herbs and spices

mixed dried herbs
freeze-dried basil
chilli flakes
paprika

How long can I keep this before it kills me?

HOW LONG CAN I KEEP THINGS?

Raw meat	1 day in the fridge.
Bacon	2 to 3 days in the fridge.
Cooked meat: cooked chicken/ham, etc	3 days maximum in the fridge.
Eggs	1 month from lay date (usually the use-by date on the egg).
Milk	2–3 days once opened. If unopened, see 'best-before' date.
Butter and margarine	6 weeks
Cheese	1 week once opened, 2 weeks unopened. Keep cheese wrapped.
Onions and potatoes	1 week, best out of the fridge and in a dark place.
Green vegetables	1 week in fridge.
Carrots, parsnips, etc.	1 week in fridge.
Salad, lettuce, cucumber, tomatoes, peppers, etc.	1 week in fridge.
Leftovers	ONLY the day after the food has been cooked. All kinds of nasties can begin to lurk there.

'Sell-by dates' are when the store needs to sell things by. 'Use-by dates' are indications that you should not be eating them after said date.

Here are some basic guidelines that should help you avoid making yourself ill:

HOW DO I KNOW IF SOMETHING IS PAST IT?

Cheese	Green mould on the surface.
Potatoes	Skin is turning green and excessive 'ears'.
Yogurts	Lid 'puffing up'. If opened, the smell changes and it tastes 'sharp'.
Bread	Mould around the crust.
Vegetables	Originally crisp, vegetables now soft and soggy, e.g. 'bendy' carrots.
Red meat	Colour changes to brown or khaki colour.
Chicken	Begins to smell bad.

Reheating

Take care when reheating food that you **heat it thoroughly.** It should be 'piping hot'. This means all the food should be steaming and the plate needs a cloth to get it out of the microwave.

To reheat a plate of food in microwave, **cover it with cling film and place on a high heat** for approximately 3½ mins in a 600watt microwave. However, refer to point above if you are unsure.

Best not to reheat pork, bacon or shellfish.

Storing stuff

Keep things covered in the fridge. This helps things last longer and rules out cross-contamination, especially if you share a fridge with someone who leaves disgusting things in there! If you cook a meal one day, eat any leftovers the next day and not after that.

Be very careful with rice. Cool it quickly and place it in the fridge. Use plastic boxes to store things, like cheese, in the fridge. Cling film is a wonderful invention.

Don't keep opened tins in the fridge; a chemical reaction occurs, affecting the food, once the tin is open to the air. Transfer any excess to a bowl and cover with cling film.

Keep potatoes out of the fridge and in a cool, dark place. This can be inside a cupboard, as it stops them going green so quickly.

Seven steps to success

Here are some things that will help you enjoy cooking and hopefully minimise discouraging failures.

1 **Plan what you will eat** and **shop for the week,** all in one go. This saves time and money, as you will not buy stuff you don't need. At the back of the book you will find sample menus for a week. Once you are used to using these, you can make your own menus and shopping lists.

2 **Start by cooking the easy things** you know and like, if you are not a confident cook.

3 **Read the recipe** all the way through, before you begin, in order to get a clear idea of what you are doing.

4 **Prepare all the ingredients** before you begin cook. For example, don't try to chop vegetables whilst you are frying other things.

5 **Avoid trying something new** when you are cooking for others.

6 **Avoid having the heat source too high**, either in the oven or on the top of the cooker.

7 **Try to keep clean** your cooking area, your section of the fridge, etc.

What do I do if...

...everything I cook in the oven is burnt or undercooked?

It could be, that if you have an older oven, the thermostat is not working quite as well as it should. Don't give up, just adjust by raising or lowering the temperature you set it to. Also, the temperatures in some ovens can vary a great deal, depending on which shelf you put your food on. Where possible, use middle shelves. Check what kind of oven you have: Centigrade, Centigrade fan oven or Fahrenheit oven. Then check the temperature on the recipe.

...I don't have a microwave to defrost food?

Keep the food in the freezer bag and place in cold water. Don't use boiling water. The best thing is to plan ahead, take food out of the freezer and leave in the fridge overnight to defrost.

...everything I cook on top of the cooker is burnt?

Either you need to keep the heat turned down, or just keep an eye on things. You can't go off and ring your mates whilst trying to cook.

...I have made things too spicy?

With Chilli Con Carne, just try adding another tin of tomatoes. With a curry, peel and cut a potato into four and add to the curry. Simmer for 10 minutes and remove potato.

...I don't have a lid for my casserole dish?

Cover the dish with tin foil.

...I don't have a pastry brush?

Use your fingers or a spoon.

If you have any other questions, why not ask Joy at: **www.noshbooks.com** or see Joy's book **"101 Questions Students Ask About Cooking"**.

Veggies

Boiling

Generally, most vegetables need to be cooked in just enough water to cover them.

1. Bring the water to the boil.
2. Once boiling, add the vegetables and a little salt and simmer gently with the lid on the pan. If you keep the source of the heat low, you will preserve a little more of the nutrition in the vegetables.

BOILING TIMES

Swedes and turnips	2–3cm chunks	20–25 mins
Potatoes	2–3cm chunks	10–15 mins
Parsnips, carrots	cut into 2cm rings	10–15 mins
Cauliflower	broken into little trees	10 mins
Broccoli	broken into little trees	5 mins
Green beans	cut off the stalk and tail	5 mins
Spinach	take off any thick stalks	30 secs–1 min
Leeks	cut into 2cm rings	5 mins
Cabbage	cut into long thin strips	5 mins
Sugar snaps	leave as they are	2 mins
Mangetout	leave as they are	1 min

Note

For **spinach**, cook just enough to make the leaves wilt. You will only need a quarter of a mug of water in the bottom of the pan.

For **cabbage**, use half a mug of water in the pan, drain after cooking and add some butter and black pepper. Return to the pan and cook for another 2 minutes to dry the cabbage a little.

Roasting

1. Preheat the oven to 180°C fan oven/200°C/Gas 6.
2. Put the vegetables on a flat roasting/baking tray and sprinkle them with salt and olive oil. Turn them over with your hands to make sure that the oil is covering all the pieces. Set them on the tray with flat sides up. If the flat sides are on the tray itself, they will tend to stick. Sprinkle with rosemary if you wish.
3. Put in the middle of the oven for 30 minutes. Check to see if any are getting too brown, maybe the ones around the edge. Move, or turn over as necessary. Put back in the oven for another 20 minutes. You can put a mix of veg in (see photo below). If you are roasting individual veg, see timings below:

ROASTING TIMES

Potatoes	cut into 5–6cm chunks	40–50 mins
Butternut squash	peel, cut into 5–6cm chunks	30–40 mins
Parsnips	cut into 4, lengthways	40–45 mins
Sweet potatoes	peel, cut into 5–6cm chunks	40–50 mins
Onions	cut into 6 wedges	40–50 mins
Fennel	cut into 4 wedges	30–40 mins
Tomatoes	cut the skin	20–25 mins
Peppers	remove seeds and stalk, cut into large pieces	25 mins

Perfect rice every time

There are many different types of rice to buy. I would recommend that you use basmati. It is slightly more expensive than long-grain or quick-cook rice, but has a much better flavour and texture than the cheaper varieties.

| rice for 1 person | = | ½ mug rice | + | 1 mug water |

(+ 1 teaspoon of pilau rice seasoning, optional, but gives a yummy flavour.)

1. Using a pan with a lid, bring the water to the boil, add the seasoning and stir until it has dissolved.

2. Add the rice and stir once. Bring back to the boil. Once boiling, turn down the heat to very low, so that the rice simmers gently. Put the lid on the pan and cook for approximately 15 minutes. Do not stir whilst the rice is cooking, or you will make it sticky. The rice should be cooked once the water has disappeared. Check occasionally to see if the water has boiled away.

3. Test the rice once the water has boiled away. If the rice is still too crunchy and the water has all gone, then you have boiled it too quickly. Add a little more water, replace the lid and cook for another 5 minutes.

How to cook pasta

There are innumerable kinds of pasta to choose from in the shops, made from different ingredients. Most will have instructions on the packets as to how to cook them. Just in case you have lost the packet, here are some general guidelines:

Spaghetti

1. Use the guide above to measure the quantities required for 1–4 people. Boil sufficient water in a pan to cover the spaghetti whilst cooking.

2. Once the water is boiling, lower the spaghetti sticks into the water. Once the half that is in the water has softened slightly, push the other half in. Simmer for 6–8 minutes.

3. Test one piece to see if it is cooked. Drain the water off and add one teaspoon of butter or olive oil. Mix around and this will stop the spaghetti sticking together.

Most other pastas

Again, boil enough water to cover the pasta. Once the water is boiling, add the pasta. **One mug of dried pasta is plenty for one person with a very healthy appetite.** Simmer for the appropriate time, drain and add butter or olive oil to prevent the pasta sticking together.

Here is a guide, but it still depends on the thickness of the pasta:
Tagliatelle - the stuff that comes in little nests. 4–5 minutes.
Spaghetti - 6 minutes, depending how thick the spaghetti is.
Radiatore - looks like little radiators. 10 minutes.
Fusilli - little twists. 6–8 minutes.
Penne - little tubes, vary in size. 10–12 minutes.
Conchiglie - little shells. 6–8 minutes.
Macaroni - 12–15 minutes.
Farfalle - looks like little bows. 6–8 minutes.

Use medium or large potatoes. Always make a cut in the skin with a knife before baking, or it may explode in the oven or the microwave. You will only get the crisp jackets if you cook the potato in the oven. Timing depends on the size of the potato.

Oven baked — Preheat the oven to 200°C fan oven/220°C/Gas 7, bake for 50–60 minutes.

Microwave and oven — Preheat the oven to 200°C fan oven/220°C/Gas 7. Cook in the microwave on full power for 5 minutes and then in the oven for 30 minutes.

Microwave — 7–10 minutes on full power.

Fillings

When the potato is cooked, cut it open and add a little butter to moisten, then add any of the following suggestions:

1 **The simplest**—Baked beans and/or grated cheese.

2 **Tuna Sweetcorn and mayo**—Mix together ½ x 185g tin of tuna with 1 tablespoon of mayo and ½ x 340g tin sweetcorn, season well. (If you double these quantities you have some sandwich filling for the next day.)

3 **Cottage cheese**—½ x 250g tub of cottage cheese, mixed with 3 chopped spring onions and 6 or 7 defrosted cooked shrimps. You could add a chopped tomato if you wish. (Use the rest of the tub of cottage cheese in sandwiches.)

4 **Cooked chicken and mayonnaise**—If you have roasted a chicken, (see page 88) chop up a portion of it and add 1 tablespoon of mayo + ½ teaspoon mustard.

5 **Smoked mackerel**—You can buy this quite cheaply. It is already cooked and in sealed bags. Take the skin off one piece and gently break up the fish, add 2 chopped spring onions and 1 tablespoon of mayonnaise or crème fraîche. (Keep the rest of the fish covered in cling film and use in Smoked Mackerel Pasta Salad, see page 50.)

6 **Crispy bacon and hard-boiled eggs**—Hard boil 2 eggs (see page 26), take off the shells and chop them up. Grill 2 rashers of streaky bacon and chop them up also. Mix together. You can add 1 tablespoon mayo and/or ½ x 340g tin sweetcorn if you wish. (If you are making a dish using bacon, e.g. Salsa Salad p 47, then just keep a couple of rashers for this recipe.)

sandwiches sandwiches
sandwiches sandwiches
sandwiches sandwiches
sandwiches sandwiches
sandwiches sandwiches
sandwiches sandwiches
sandwiches sandwiches
sandwiches sandwiches
sandwiches sandwiches
sandwiches sandwiches
sandwiches sandwiches

One way to make sandwiches more interesting is to vary the bread you use. Try to avoid white bread all the time, as all the good stuff has been taken out and some not so good stuff added in. Choose different kinds of wholemeal or granary loaves, bread buns or pitta breads.

Bacon and banana
Grill or fry 3 slices of streaky bacon, until crisp. Whilst it is still hot, put in the sandwich with a sliced banana. Squash the top slice on to keep everything in.

Cottage cheese with tomatoes or cucumber
Chop a tomato, or a 4cm piece of cucumber, quite small. Mix together with ½ x 250g pot of cottage cheese. Season well.

Egg mayo
Hard boil 2 eggs, see page 26. Rinse them under cold water, take off the shells and chop them up with a knife. Mix them together with 1 tablespoon mayo and season with salt and pepper.

Tuna with hard-boiled eggs
Drain a 185g tin tuna. Put half in a bowl. Hard boil 2 eggs, see page 26. Peel and chop and add to the bowl. Chop 2 spring onions and add to the bowl with 1 tablespoon of mayo. Mix together and season well.

BLT
Fry 3 rashers of streaky bacon until they are crispy. Spread one slice of bread with mayo. Add 2 lettuce leaves and one sliced tomato. Season with pepper, the bacon has enough saltiness. Add the bacon on top and the final slice of bread.

Peanut butter and bananas
Spread a liberal amount of peanut butter on one slice. Spread jam or honey on top. Slice a banana and pile it in. Put the second slice of bread on top and squash down.

Cottage cheese with bananas
Spread the bread with a liberal amount of honey or jam. Top with cottage cheese. Slice a banana and pile into the sandwich. Top with the other slice of bread.

Chicken and mayo with lettuce
If you have roasted a chicken and have some spare, cut it into small pieces. Spread mayo over one slice of bread and add the lettuce. Season with salt and pepper. Add the chicken on top and place the other slice of bread on top.

Scrambled eggs, cheese and tomato
Grate ½ mug cheese. Chop a tomato quite finely. Heat a little butter in a small non-stick saucepan, add the tomatoes and fry for 1 minute. Add 2 eggs and cook until they begin to set. Add the cheese and cook for 30 seconds. Season well and make the sandwich whilst the eggs are still hot.

Stuff on toast

Cheese on toast
with a little something extra.

1. Very lightly toast the bread under a hot grill, since you will return it to the grill later to cook the cheese.

2. Butter the toast. At this stage you can add things to go under the cheese, such as ham, pickle, Marmite, or sliced tomatoes.

3. Slice or grate the cheese and place on top. Make sure the cheese covers the edges of the toast; it will protect the corners of the bread from being burned. Use a slotted turner to put the toast back under the grill.

4. Cook until the cheese begins to bubble.

Eggie bread
1. Break an egg into a mug and beat with a fork. Pour out onto a plate.

2. Dip one side of a thick slice of bread into the egg, quickly turn over and let the other side soak up the rest of the egg.

3. Put a 2cm cube of butter in a frying pan and heat gently until the butter starts to bubble.

4. Add the bread and cook, turning over to brown both sides.

5. Serve with beans, HP or tomato sauce. To make it into breakfast, serve with honey, or maple syrup and sliced fruit.

Beans on toast with egg on top
Toast the bread, heat the beans and then fry or poach the eggs (page 26). Great with HP sauce.

Welsh Rarebit
½ mug grated **Cheddar cheese**
2 teaspoons **flour**
½ mug **milk**
½ teaspoon **mustard**
1 teaspoon **Worcestershire Sauce**
1 **egg yolk**
2cm cube **butter**

1. Without the heat on, put the grated cheese and the flour in a small saucepan and mix well.

2. Add the rest of the ingredients and mix well.

3. Heat slowly until the mixture thickens and is hot. Serve on a thick slice of toast.

Garlic bread
This works best with medium-sized bread sticks.

1. Finely chop 1 garlic clove, and mix together with about 3cm cube of butter. You could add 1 teaspoon of freeze-dried chives at this point if you wish.

2. Make diagonal cuts in the bread stick, but not quite all the way through.

3. Push the garlic butter into the cuts in the bread. Don't use loads, because it will be very greasy if you do.

4. Wrap the bread stick in foil and bake in the oven for 7–8 minutes (200°C fan oven/220°C/Gas 7).

Eggs

Boil

1. Using a small pan, fill ⅔ full with water and bring to the boil.
2. Lower the egg into the pan on a spoon.
3. Simmer briskly for 3 minutes for a very runny egg, 5 minutes and you will still be able to dip your 'soldiers' in the runny yolk, 12 minutes and it will be hard-boiled.

Poach

1. Using a small pan, or frying pan, half fill with water and add a good pinch of salt. Bring to the boil, then turn down until the water is only just moving.
2. Break the egg into a mug or cup and gently pour into the water. Do not stir or turn the heat up, just let it cook gently. It will take 2–4 minutes, depending on the size of the egg.
3. Once the egg has gone opaque, gently lift out with a slotted turner and let the water drain from it.

Fry

1. Heat 2 teaspoons butter in the frying pan until the butter just bubbles.
2. Break the egg into a mug and then gently pour into the frying pan.
3. Cook on medium/low heat, until the egg is set.
4. Using a slotted turner, turn the egg over half-way through cooking, if you want 'easy over' hard yolk.

Scramble

1. Using a small milk pan, preferably non-stick, add 2 teaspoons butter and heat gently until the butter bubbles.
2. Break the egg into the pan and add salt and pepper. Stir slowly, breaking up the egg yolk.
3. When the egg is almost set, take off the heat. The egg will continue to cook in its own heat. If you cook it too long, it will become rubbery.
4. You can add grated cheese and/or chopped tomatoes half-way through the cooking.

Omelettes

Instructions for a basic omelette for 1 person

1. Put two or three eggs in a mug and beat well with a fork, adding two tablespoons of water.

2. Switch on the grill to full heat to warm up.

3. Melt about a dessertspoon of butter in the frying pan. Once it begins to 'bubble', pour the egg mixture into the pan.

4. As the egg begins to set on the bottom of the pan, gently move the set egg with fish slice and allow the runny egg to take its place. Do this with two or three sweeping movements; don't stir, or you will get scrambled egg. If you are making double quantity, repeat this process once more.

5. While there is still a little runny egg on the top, take off the heat, add whatever filling you want, top with cheese (not essential) and place the frying pan under the hot grill. The omelette should rise. Once it is browned on the top, remove from the grill and turn out onto a plate. Serve with salad, garlic bread or baked potatoes.

Suggested fillings – cheese, tomato, mushrooms, fried onions, crispy grilled bacon cut into pieces, cooked chicken, ham or any combination of these ingredients.

Sauces

This is a simple, useful and versatile **basic sauce**. You can use this sauce as a pasta sauce, **for veggie bakes**, **lasagna** and **cauliflower cheese**.

Quick Cheese Sauce

1 mug grated **cheese**
1 tablespoon **flour**
1cm cube **butter**

1 mug **milk**
⅛ teaspoon **paprika**
salt and **pepper**

1. Without the heat on, put the grated cheese into a saucepan, add the flour, salt, pepper and paprika and stir well.

2. Add the milk and butter. Put on a low heat and bring to the boil, stirring all the time. The sauce should thicken.

Here are a couple of sauces that you can **use on pasta**, or to accompany other foods:

Piquant Tomato Sauce

1 **t**ablespoon of **oil** to fry
1 **onion**, sliced
400g **tin tomatoes**
1 teaspoon **black pepper**

1 tablespoon **tomato purée**
1 tablespoon **white wine vinegar**
1 teaspoon **sugar**

1. Heat the oil in a saucepan and fry the onions until they become soft. Add the tomatoes.

2. Add the rest of the ingredients and bring to the boil. Simmer for 2–3 minutes.

3. Blitz with a hand-held blender if you have one, or use as it is.

Pepper Sauce

1½ red **peppers**, chopped
½ **onion**, sliced
1 **clove garlic**, chopped

1 tablespoon **cream**
½ teaspoon **sugar**
salt and **pepper**

1. Fry the peppers, onions, and garlic in a saucepan over a medium heat for 5–8 minutes, until they are really soft.

2. Add the sugar and cream and mix.

3. Use a hand-held blender to liquidise, or leave as it is.

4. Add the cream and season well with salt and freshly ground black pepper. You can add half a teaspoon of chilli powder if you like.

fast food

Home from uni and in a rush to get out? Here are some quick and easy things for you to try.

fast food

Tuna and Mushroom Spaghetti

Don't stir the tuna too much or it will become mushy.

£1.15 /PERSON

2

2-3

PREP 25 MINS

1½ portions **spaghetti** (see page 19)

1 tablespoon **oil** to fry

1 small **onion**, sliced

5–6 **mushrooms**, sliced

½ mug **frozen peas**, defrosted

3 tablespoons **Greek yogurt**

185g can **tuna in oil**, drained

juice of a ½ **lemon**

½ mug grated **Parmesan**

1 dessertspoon **dried chives**

salt and **pepper**

1. Cook the spaghetti (see page 19). Drain and return to the pan.

2. While the spaghetti is cooking, heat a little oil in a wok, fry the onion until it begins to soften. Add the mushrooms and the peas and cook for 1 minute. Season well.

3. Take the pan off the heat and add the yogurt, tuna, lemon juice, grated Parmesan and the chives. Stir gently. Add to the drained spaghetti. Stir gently and serve.

Beefy Mince and Pasta Bake

Very simple to make and share with flatmates. It is OK reheated in the microwave, but best eaten straight away.

1½ mugs **pasta**

1 tablespoon **oil** to fry

1 **onion**, chopped

2 cloves **garlic**, finely chopped

400g pack of beef **mince** or Quorn

1 **beef/vegetable stock cube**

295g tin of Campbell's **condensed tomato soup** (undiluted)

1 teaspoon **freeze-dried basil**

salt and **pepper**

½ mug grated **cheese**

£1.10 /PERSON

2

2-3

PREP 10 MINS

COOK 25 MINS

V OPTION

1. Preheat oven to 200°C fan oven/220°C/Gas 7.
2. Cook the pasta (see page 19).
3. Heat a little oil in a frying pan or wok. Fry the onion and garlic until soft.
4. Add the mince and cook until no longer pink.
5. Add the stock cube, tomato soup, herbs and salt and pepper.
6. Drain the pasta well and add to the meat mixture. Transfer to a casserole dish.
7. Top with grated cheese and cook for 20–25 minutes. The top should be browned.

Lemony Couscous Chicken

If you have roasted a chicken, you could use any leftovers in this recipe. Add at stage 3, but you will only need to heat it for 30 seconds at that stage, then go on to the next stages. It should be thoroughly heated by stage 6.

£2.10 /PERSON

2

2

PREP 25 MINS

1 mug **couscous**

rind of 1 **lemon**, finely grated + the juice of half a **lemon**

2 mugs boiling **water**

50g **butter** (measure by packet)

1 **onion**, thinly sliced

1 **red pepper**, diced

1 **clove garlic**, finely chopped

1 large **chicken breast,** cut into small pieces

6 **mushrooms**, chopped

1 teaspoon **sugar**

½ x 100g **pine nuts**

1 fat **red chilli**, sliced thinly

1 teaspoon **freeze-dried chives**

1. Place the couscous, lemon rind and juice in a bowl. Pour the 2 cups of boiling water over it. Stir, cover with a plate or cling film, and leave to stand for about 5 minutes.

2. Heat the butter in a pan and add the onions, peppers and garlic. Fry until the onions are soft.

3. Add the chicken pieces and cook until they are no longer pink.

4. Add the mushrooms and the sugar, cook for 1 minute.

5. Add the pine nuts and the chilli. Just allow to heat through.

6. Stir in the couscous and the chives.

Quesidillas

Quesidillas can be varied. Here are the basic instructions and one set of ingredients which can be used. If you are vegetarian, obviously leave out the meat and add other vegetables of your choice. For quesidillas, it is best to buy the soft, flour tortillas.

400g can of **cannellini beans**

1 **chicken breast** or 200g beef mince

2 tablespoons **oil** to fry

1 **onion**, chopped finely

1 **pepper**, chopped

5 **mushrooms**, sliced

1 tablespoon **tomato purée**, mixed with 4 tablespoons water

salt and **pepper**

8 **tortilla** (soft flour) **wraps**

1. Wash the beans well and leave to drain.

2. Fry the whole chicken breast in a little oil until cooked through (no longer pink inside). Take out of the pan and leave to stand.

3. Fry the onion until it begins to brown, then add the pepper and mushrooms. (If you use beef mince, add now and cook until no longer pink). Cook for another 3–4 minutes. Take off the heat.

4. Cut the chicken into thin strips and add to the vegetable mix, along with the beans and tomato purée. Season well with salt and pepper.

5. Put the grill on to heat up.

6. Wash the frying pan. Butter one side of the tortilla wraps. Put the freshly cleaned pan on to heat up. Put one of the wraps, butter side down, in the pan. Put ¼ of the filling onto the wrap and spread it out, then place the other wrap, butter side up, on the top of the filling. Now place under the grill until the butter begins to brown.

7. Slide onto a plate and cut into wedges. Serve with salsa (see page 137) and/or soured cream.

Hawaiian Risotto

Make the leftover pineapple into a smoothie or just eat. Tinned fruit still has lots of good stuff in it.

½ mug **rice** + ½ teaspoon **pilau rice** seasoning

1 tablespoon **oil** to fry

1 **egg**, beaten

1 small **onion**, chopped

2–3 **mushrooms**, sliced

¼ **red pepper**, sliced

2 **pineapple slices**, cut into pieces

1 teaspoon **soy sauce**

1 slice of **cooked ham**, cut into pieces

1 **tomato**, cut into chunks

1 teaspoon **freeze-dried coriander** leaves

salt and **pepper**

1. Cook the rice with the pilau rice seasoning (see page 18).
2. Heat a little oil in a frying pan, add the egg to it, and allow it to spread thinly over the base of the pan. It will cook in less than a minute. Once cooked, take out of the pan, cut into strips and leave to one side.
3. Add a little more oil to the pan and fry the onions until they are soft.
4. Add the mushrooms and peppers and cook for 30 seconds.
5. Add the cooked rice, pineapple, soy sauce, ham, egg, tomato and coriander leaves. Heat through gently. Season with salt and pepper.

Creamy Chicken

Using chicken breast makes this recipe is a little more expensive, but is very quick and easy to cook.

£2.50 /PERSON

1

2

PREP 20 MINS

1 tablespoon **oil** to fry

1 **onion**, sliced

1 clove **garlic**, finely chopped

2 **chicken breasts**, cut into pieces

5–6 **mushrooms**, sliced

½ mug **double cream** (¼ pint)

1 **chicken stock cube**, crumbled

1 teaspoon **freeze-dried basil**

1 mug **basmati rice**

1 teaspoon **pilau rice** seasoning

1. Put the rice on to cook with the pilau seasoning (see page 18).
2. Heat a little oil in a frying pan and fry the onions and garlic until soft.
3. Add the chicken breast. Cook on a high heat until the chicken is no longer pink. Add the mushrooms and cook for 2 minutes.
4. Add the cream and the stock cube. Cook gently for 5–10 minutes, stirring occasionally.
5. Add the basil and cook for one minute.
6. Serve with rice.

Chicken Risotto

This is a good way to stretch one chicken breast to make enough for two people.

2cm cube **butter**

1 **onion**, chopped

1 **chicken breast** or 2–3 small chicken breast fillets

4 **mushrooms**, sliced

¼ **red pepper,** chopped

⅓ mug **rice**, can be risotto or basmati

½ **chicken stock cube**, crumbled

½ teaspoon **mild curry paste**

1 mug **water**

165g tin **sweetcorn**

1 teaspoon **freeze-dried chives**

£1.25 /PERSON

2

2

PREP 15 MINS

COOK 20 MINS

1. Heat the butter in a frying pan and fry the onion until soft.

2. Cut the chicken into bite-sized pieces, add to the pan and fry for 2–3 minutes until the outside is no longer pink.

3. Add the mushroom and pepper.

4. Add the rice (uncooked), stock cube, curry paste and water. Simmer gently for 20 minutes, stirring from time to time. Add more water if the mixture has dried up before the rice is cooked. There should be very little liquid left when the dish is finished.

5. Add the sweetcorn and chives, heat through and serve.

Tuna and Pasta Bake

You can use different condensed soups; celery or chicken, for example.

2 mugs **pasta**

185g tin **tuna steak**, drained of oil

295g tin Campbell's **condensed cream of mushroom soup**

2 packets of **crisps**

½ mug grated **cheese**

£1.60 /PERSON

1

2-3

PREP 10 MINS

COOK 20 MINS

1. Preheat the oven to 200°C fan oven/220°C/Gas 7.
2. Cook the pasta (see page 19).
3. Drain and place back in the saucepan. Add the tuna and condensed soup (do not dilute the soup). Mix together.
4. Transfer to a casserole dish.
5. Crush the crisps in the bag, mix with the grated cheese, and sprinkle on top of the mixture in the casserole dish.
6. Cook in the oven for 20 minutes until the cheese and crisps are browned.

Salmon Pasta

You can sometimes buy packs of small pieces of salmon. They are much cheaper and would be excellent for this dish.

2 small bunches of **tagliatelle pasta**

1 small piece of **salmon**

1 tablespoon **olive oil** to fry

3 **spring onions**, chopped

2 tablespoons of **double cream**

1 teaspoon **freeze-dried chives**

salt and **pepper**

£1.95 /PERSON

2

1

PREP 15 MINS

1. Cook the tagliatelle. It should only take about 3–4 minutes to cook (see page 19). Leave to drain.

2. Fry the salmon in a little olive oil (if you have a small piece it should only take 2–3 minutes each side). Add the spring onions to the pan towards the end of the cooking time and allow them to brown a little.

3. Remove the pan from the heat and gently break up the salmon. Add the cream and the chives and return to the heat. As soon as the cream begins to bubble, add the pasta and stir everything together. Allow the pasta to heat through. This should take around 1 minute.

4. Season well with salt and pepper.

Bacon and Egg Pasta

As soon as the hard-boiled eggs are cooked, drain and run under cold water. This stops them from going black around the yolk.

£1.15 /PERSON

2

2

PREP 25 MINS

2 **eggs**, hard-boiled

1 mug **pasta**

1 tablespoon **oil** to fry

4 rashers **bacon**

3 **mushrooms**, sliced

2 tablespoons **mayonnaise**

1 tablespoon **olive oil**

salt and **pepper**

3 **spring onions**, chopped

1. Cook the pasta and the eggs in the same pan. Boil the water and add the eggs first and then the pasta a few minutes later, so that it does not overcook; i.e. eggs for 10 minutes, then pasta and eggs for a further 5 minutes.

2. Fry the bacon until crisp and remove from the pan. Add the mushrooms and fry until browned.

3. Cut the bacon into bite-size pieces.

4. Mix the oil and mayonnaise together.

5. Drain the pasta and eggs and run under cold water. Take the shells off the eggs and cut each into four.

6. Mix everything together and serve with a little green salad.

Cold Chicken and Nut Salad

You can use left-over roast chicken for this recipe. If you have left-over crème fraîche, you can make it into a dip (see page 135) and make some carrot sticks to go with it.

£1.40 /PERSON

1

2

PREP 15 MINS

1 large **chicken breast**

1 green **eating apple**

2 tablespoons **mayonnaise**

2 tablespoons **crème fraîche**

1 teaspoon **freeze-dried chives**

4 **celery sticks**, sliced

6–8 **walnuts** or pecans, cut in half

½ mug **raisins**

green salad to serve

1. Cut the chicken into bite-sized pieces. Heat a little oil in a frying pan, add the chicken, and cook on a medium heat until the chicken is no longer pink.

2. Cut the apple into small pieces, leaving the skin on.

3. Mix the mayonnaise and crème fraîche with the chives, celery, nuts and raisins.

4. Mix everything together and serve with green salad and crusty bread.

Cold Chicken Salad

Any leftovers can be eaten cold or used in sandwiches the next day.

£1.70 /PERSON

1

2

PREP 15 MINS

1 tablespoon **oil** to fry

1 **red onion**, chopped

2 **chicken breasts,** cut into small pieces

1 teaspoon **soy sauce**

juice of ½ **lime**

1 clove **garlic**, finely chopped

1 teaspoon **Korma curry paste**

2 teaspoons **brown sugar**

1 teaspoon **freeze-dried coriander**

salt and **pepper**

1. Heat a little oil in the frying pan and fry the onion until soft.
2. Add the chicken and fry until the meat is no longer pink.
3. Add the rest of the ingredients. Cook for 2 minutes and leave to cool.
4. Serve with salad.

Shrimp Couscous Salad

You need to add plenty of tasty things to couscous, plus some kind of dressing or sauce.

£3.35 /PERSON

1

1

PREP 10 MINS

½ mug **couscous**

1 mug **boiling water**

1 **tomato**

2 **spring onions**

¼ **red or green pepper**, chopped coarsely

1 teaspoon **olive oil**

juice of ½ **lemon**

1 teaspoon **freeze-dried chives**

¼ x 300g pack **frozen shrimps**, defrosted

2.5cm **cucumber**, cut into cubes

1. Put the couscous in a bowl and add the boiling water. Cover with a plate. Leave to stand for about 4 minutes. All the water should be absorbed into the couscous.

2. Chop the tomato, spring onion and pepper into small pieces.

3. To make the dressing, mix the oil, lemon, garlic and chives together.

4. Mix all the ingredients together and serve with a green salad.

Tuna Salad

You can add other ingredients: cucumber, tomatoes or some fresh chilli to spice it up a little.

1 mug **pasta**

1 mug **frozen peas**

4–5 **spring onions**, chopped

1 **red pepper**, chopped

3 tablespoons **mayonnaise**

185g tin **tuna**, drained of oil

1 teaspoon **freeze-dried chives**

salt and **pepper**

£1.60 /PERSON

1

2

PREP 15 MINS

1. Cook pasta (see page 19), add the peas in the same pan and simmer for a further 2 minutes. Drain and cool.

2. Flake the tuna, season with salt and pepper.

3. Mix all the ingredients together.

4. Serve with lettuce and tomatoes.

Potato Salad

Serve with sausages, cold meats and green salad. Ideal with barbecue food.

2 **medium-sized potatoes**, chopped into small cubes

3 dessertspoons **mayonnaise**

2 tablespoons **crème fraîche**

4–5 **spring onions**, chopped

1 teaspoon **freeze-dried chives**

1 teaspoon **freeze-dried mint**

salt and **pepper**

1. Boil the potatoes for 10 minutes. Drain and leave to cool.
2. Mix the mayonnaise and crème fraîche together. Add the chives and mint.
3. Add the onions and mix everything together. Season well.

Salsa Salad

As soon as the eggs are cooked, remember to rinse them under cold water, as this stops the yolks going black around the edges.

2 hard-boiled **eggs** (see page 26)

2 medium **potatoes** or 8 small new potatoes

4 large **tomatoes**

3 **spring onions**, chopped

1 clove **garlic**, chopped finely

1 teaspoon **freeze-dried chives**

juice of ½ a **lemon**

2 tablespoons **olive oil**

4 rashers of **unsmoked bacon**

salt and **pepper**

½ **curly leaf lettuce**

£1.55 /PERSON

2

2

PREP 20 MINS

1. Peel the eggs and cut each one into 4 pieces.

2. Wash and cut the potatoes into bite-sized chunks. Put them in boiling water and then simmer for 10–15 minutes. Drain and leave to cool.

3. Make the salsa, using 2 of the tomatoes. Chop them into quite small pieces. Put in a bowl and add the chopped spring onions, garlic, chives, lemon juice and olive oil. Season with salt and pepper and mix well.

4. Fry or grill the bacon until it is crisp, then cut into bite-size pieces.

5. Cut the remaining tomatoes into ¼'s.

6. Wash and drain the lettuce and arrange on the two plates. Arrange the tomatoes, potatoes, bacon and eggs on the top. Pour the salsa over the top and serve.

Hot Potato Salad

No need to peel or scrub the potatoes, just wash them. This can be a meal in itself if served with green salad.

£1.40 /PERSON

2

2

PREP 15 MINS

3 **potatoes**, or 6 new potatoes, cut into bite-sized chunks

1 tablespoon **oil** to fry

4–5 **mushrooms**, sliced

4 rashers of **bacon**

4–5 **spring onions**, chopped

1 teaspoon **freeze-dried parsley**

Dressing

2 tablespoons **olive oil**

1 teaspoon **wholegrain mustard**

1 tablespoon **white wine vinegar**

1. Put the potatoes in boiling water, simmer for 10 minutes and drain.

2. Heat a little oil in a frying pan and fry the mushrooms until they are browned. Set to one side.

3. Fry bacon until brown and then cut into small pieces.

4. Mix all the bacon, mushrooms, onions, parsley and potatoes, taking care not to break the potatoes up too much.

5. Mix the dressing ingredients together. Pour over the top.

Fruity Tuna Salad

Take care not to mix the tuna too vigorously as it will end up very mushy.

227g can **pineapple chunks**, drained of juice

185g **tuna**, drained of oil

2 hard-boiled **eggs**, peeled and quartered

2 **sticks celery**, sliced

4 **spring onions**, chopped

1 small **clove garlic**, finely chopped

½ mug **pecans**, each cut in half

salt and **pepper**

Dressing

2 tablespoons of **olive oil**

juice of a **lemon**

1 **little gem lettuce**

£1.60/PERSON

2

2

PREP 20 MINS

1. Mix the salad ingredients together. Divide between 2 plates.

2. Mix the dressing ingredients together and drizzle over each plate.

3. Serve with little gem lettuce.

Smoked Mackerel Pasta Salad

You can buy cooked, smoked mackerel in vacuum packs. Usually found with the fresh fish in the supermarket. If unopened, they will keep in the fridge for quite a while.

£1.60 /PERSON

1

2-3

PREP 20 MINS

1½ mugs **pasta**

½ x 300g pack **green beans**, trimmed and cut in ½

2 tablespoons **crème fraîche**

1 tablespoon **mayo**

1 teaspoon **freeze-dried chives**

zest and juice of ½ **lemon**

salt and **pepper**

250g pack **cooked, smoked mackerel**

¼ **cucumber**, chopped

2 **spring onions**, chopped

1. Put the pasta on to boil (see page 19). Add the beans 5 minutes before the end of the cooking time. Once cooked, drain, run under a cold tap and place in a bowl.

2. Mix together the crème fraîche, mayo, chives, lemon zest, juice and salt and pepper. Add to the pasta and mix.

3. Peel the skin off the backs of the mackerel fillets and then gently flake the fish. Add to the bowl, along with the cucumber and onions. Mix gently and serve.

Lime Tuna with Couscous

Don't stir tinned tuna too much as it tends to go mushy. Allow it to stay in recognizable pieces. To deseed a cucumber, cut in half lengthways and scoop out the seeds with a small spoon.

£1.50 /PERSON

2

2

PREP 20 MINS

¾ mug **couscous**

1½ mugs boiling **water** + 1 **vegetable stock cube**

zest of a **lime**

juice of a **lime**

1 teaspoon **sugar**

salt and **pepper**

2 tablespoons **olive oil**

185g tin **tuna**

250g pack of **cherry tomatoes**, halved

7cm piece of **cucumber**, halved, deseeded and thinly sliced

½ x 340g tin **sweetcorn**

1. Place the couscous and lemon zest in a bowl and pour over the boiling water and crumbled vegetable stock cube. Put a plate over the top to keep the heat in and leave to stand for 5 minutes.

2. Mix together the lime zest, lime juice, sugar, salt and pepper and olive oil to make a dressing.

3. Once the couscous is cooked, add the drained tuna, tomatoes, cucumber, sweetcorn and the dressing to the couscous. Stir and serve.

broke but hungry

Waiting for pay day, or is the loan rapidly running out? Here are some inexpensive dishes to keep the hunger pangs at bay.

broke but hungry

Italian Soup

The ingredients for this soup may seem a little complicated. Don't worry if you don't have them all. The celery and the spinach can be left out if you wish.

£0.85 /PERSON

1

2-3

PREP 20 MINS

V

2cm cube **butter**

1 onion, **chopped**

1 small **potato**, diced

1 **carrot**, diced

½ **red pepper**, chopped

1–2 **celery sticks**, sliced

2 cloves **garlic**, finely chopped

400g **tin of chopped tomatoes**

1 tablespoon **tomato purée**

3 mugs **water**

1 **vegetable stock cube**, crumbled

1 portion of **spaghetti** (see page 19), broken into pieces

2 pieces frozen **spinach**

1 teaspoon **freeze-dried basil**

salt and **pepper**

1. Melt the butter in a saucepan, add onions, potato, carrot, pepper, celery and garlic and cook for two minutes, stirring well.

2. Add the tin of tomatoes, tomato purée, water and stock cube, bring to the boil. Simmer for 10 minutes, then add the uncooked spaghetti and simmer for a further 6 minutes.

3. Add the spinach and the basil, bring back to the boil and season well.

Vegetable Soup with Ham

The ingredients listed make a good combination, but you can use whatever vegetables you have to hand.

£0.90 /PERSON

2cm cube **butter**

½ medium **onion**, chopped

1 small **potato**, cut into cubes

1 stick of **celery**, cut into pieces

1 medium-sized **carrot**, peeled and sliced

1 dessertspoon **flour**

1½ mugs **water**

½ **vegetable** or **chicken stock cube**

¼ mug **frozen peas**

1 slice of **ham**, chopped (optional)

salt and **pepper**

1. Heat the butter in a saucepan and fry the onion for 1 minute.
2. Add the potatoes, celery and carrots and cook for about 1 minute.
3. Add flour and mix in with the vegetables already in the pan.
4. Add the water and stock cube and bring to the boil. Simmer for 10 minutes, or until the vegetables are cooked.
5. Add the peas and cook for 2 minutes.
6. Add the pieces of ham and cook for 1 minute (omit if vegetarian).
7. Serve with bread.

Sausage Soup

When reheating sausages, make sure they are heated through well and are piping hot.

£0.40 /PERSON

2

1-2

PREP 20 MINS

1 tablespoon **oil** to fry

1 small **onion**, chopped

1½ mugs **water**

1 **beef stock cube**

¼ mug **pasta**, (tagliatelle, macaroni, or small twists)

2 large **sausages** (spicy sausages work well with this recipe)

200g tin **baked bean**s

3 teaspoons **Worcestershire sauce**

salt and **pepper**

1. Heat a little oil in a saucepan and fry the onion.

2. Add the water, stock cube and pasta, bring to the boil and simmer gently for 4–5 minutes.

3. While the pasta is simmering, cook the sausages. Fry or grill them. Cut into bite-sized chunks.

4. Add the cooked sausages, beans and Worcestershire sauce. Cook for 2 minutes. Season with salt and pepper.

Pasta with Spicy Sausages

You can use vegetarian sausages with this recipe and add ½ teaspoon chilli powder at stage 4.

1 mug of **penne pasta**

1 tablespoon **oil** to fry

6 **spicy sausages**, pork, beef or vegetarian

1 small **onion**, sliced

1 clove **garlic**, chopped

400g tin **chopped tomatoes**

1 tablespoon **tomato purée**

1 teaspoon **mixed herbs**

£0.75 /PERSON

2

2

PREP 20 MINS

V OPTION

1. Cook the pasta (see page 19). Drain and return to the pan.

2. Heat a little oil in a pan and fry the sausages and then take them out of the pan. Cut them into bite-size pieces.

3. Fry the onions and garlic for 1–2 minutes.

4. Add the tinned tomatoes and tomato purée to the pan and bring to the boil. Allow to simmer for 4–5 minutes for the flavours to blend.

5. Add the sausages, herbs and the pasta to the pan and cook for a further 2–3 minutes until everything is heated through.

Lamb Cobbler

If you like the topping, it can be used, instead of potatoes, with other recipes such as Shepherd's Pie or Monday Pie.

1 dessertspoon **oil**

1 **onion,** chopped

250g packet of **mince, lamb or Quorn**

400g tin **chopped tomatoes**

1 teaspoon **mixed herbs**

salt and **pepper**

1 tablespoon **tomato purée**

Dumpling topping

1 mug **self-raising flour**

½ mug **suet**

pinch **salt**

1 teaspoon **freeze-dried basil** or **coriander**

½ mug **water**

£0.85 /PERSON

4

2-3

PREP 20 MINS

COOK 30 MINS

V OPTION

1. Preheat the oven to 180°C fan oven/200°C/Gas 6.

2. Heat a little oil in the frying pan and fry the onion until soft.

3. Add the mince and cook until the meat is no longer pink.

4. Add the tinned tomatoes, herbs, salt and pepper and tomato purée. Stir well and simmer for 5 minutes.

5. Transfer to a casserole dish.

6. To make the dumpling top, put the flour, suet, salt and herbs in a dish and stir well. Add the water slowly, until it makes a soft ball.

7. Put some flour onto a board or plate, turn out the mixture and form a ball. Cut into six pieces and form each into a ball.

8. Gently place them on the top of the meat mixture and brush the top with beaten egg or milk to help it brown. If you do not have a pastry brush, use your fingers!

9. Bake for 25–30 minutes or until the crust is browned.

Sausage Pie

There is no need to peel the potatoes for this recipe. The skins add a little extra flavour.

£0.95 /PERSON

2 large **potatoes**, diced

2cm cube **butter**

1 tablespoon **oil** to fry

4 thick pork or vegetarian **sausages**

½ **onion**, chopped

2 cloves **garlic**, finely chopped

1 **leek**, cut into 1cm slices

1 **vegetable stock cube**

½ mug **hot water**

1 teaspoon **cornflour**

salt and **pepper**

½ mug grated **cheese**

PREP 15 MINS

COOK 25 MINS

V OPTION

1. Boil the potatoes for 10 minutes, drain and return to the pan. Add the butter and shake the potatoes in the pan to distribute it. Leave to one side.

2. Put oven on to heat 180°C fan oven/200°C/Gas 6.

3. Cook the sausages in a little oil, using a frying pan or wok. When the sausages are brown, remove from pan and cut into bite-size pieces.

4. Fry the onion and garlic for 2–3 minutes in the same pan. Add the leek and cook for a further 2–3 minutes.

5. Put the vegetable stock cube in a mug and fill up to ½ with boiling water. Add to the frying pan and bring to the boil.

6. Blend the cornflour with a little cold water and then add to the frying pan, stirring well. The sauce should thicken slightly. Season well with salt and pepper.

7. Put the sausages back into the pan and stir. Pour into a casserole dish. Pile the potatoes on the top and sprinkle over with grated cheese. Bake for 25–30 minutes until the cheese has browned.

Sausage and Egg Bake

Eggs don't microwave too well. They tend to go a bit rubbery, so best to share this one.

6 herby, spicy or vegetarian **sausages**

1 **onion**, chopped finely

1 clove of **garlic**, chopped finely

400g tin of **chopped tomatoes**

1 teaspoon of **tomato purée**

400g tin of **cannellini beans**, rinsed and drained

1 teaspoon of **freeze-dried basil**

2 **eggs**

£1.00 /PERSON

2

2

PREP 15 MINS

COOK 20 MINS

V OPTION

1. Preheat the oven to 180°C fan oven/200°C/Gas 6. Grease a casserole dish.

2. Fry the sausages in a frying pan until browned. Remove from pan.

3. Fry the onion and garlic for 2–3 minutes, stirring frequently.

4. Add the tin of tomatoes and tomato purée, stir and bring to the boil. Simmer for 2–3 minutes.

5. Add the beans to the pan, continue to cook.

6. Cut each sausage into 4 and add to the pan, stir well and take off the heat. Add the basil and season well with salt and pepper.

7. Pour the mixture into the casserole dish. Break the 2 eggs over the top of the mixture.

8. Bake in the oven for 15–20 minutes until the eggs are cooked.

9. Serve with fresh, crusty bread or baked potatoes.

Spicy Risotto

If you like hot food, you can add more curry paste.

1 mug **water**

½ mug **rice**

1 teaspoon **pilau rice seasoning**

1 tablespoon **oil** to fry

1 small **onion**, chopped

1 clove **garlic**, chopped finely

125g pack of **lamb**, **beef** or **Quorn mince**

½ **lamb**, **beef** or **vegetable stock cube**

1 dessertspoon **mild curry paste**

2 **mushrooms**, sliced

¼ mug **water**

1 teaspoon **coriander leaves**

salt and **pepper**

£1.00 /PERSON

2

1

PREP 20 MINS

V OPTION

1. Cook rice with pilau rice seasoning (see page 18).

2. Heat the oil in a frying pan and fry the onion and garlic for 1 minute.

3. Add the mince and cook until it is no longer pink.

4. Add the stock, curry paste, mushrooms and the ¼ mug of water. Bring to the boil and simmer gently for 3–4 minutes until all the liquid has gone. Stir frequently.

5. Add the cooked rice to the meat mixture. Season well with salt and pepper and add the chopped coriander leaves.

Spaghetti Bolognese

'Spag Bol' is a must to master. If you cook enough sauce for two, you can either share it with a flatmate, or the next day, add either curry paste or chilli and eat with rice or baked potatoes.

£0.95 /PERSON

2

2

PREP 20 MINS

V OPTION

1 tablespoon **oil** to fry

1 **onion**, chopped

2 cloves **garlic**, chopped

250g packet of **mince**, beef, lamb or Quorn

400g tin **chopped tomatoes**

1 tablespoon **tomato purée**

4–5 **mushrooms**, sliced (optional)

1 teaspoon **sugar**

1 **beef stock cube**

1 teaspoon **freeze-dried mixed herbs**

salt and **pepper**

spaghetti to serve (see page 19)

1. Heat a little oil in a large saucepan and fry the onion and garlic for 1 minute.

2. Add the mince and cook until the meat is no longer pink.

3. Add the tin of tomatoes, tomato purée, mushrooms and sugar. Crumble the stock cube into the pan, stir well. Bring to boil, then simmer gently for 10 minutes. Add the herbs one minute before the end of the cooking time and season well with salt and pepper.

4. Put spaghetti on to cook (see page 19).

5. Drain the pasta and add a little olive oil to stop it sticking together. Serve on the plate with the Bolognese sauce on the top. You can grate Parmesan or Cheddar cheese over the top if you like.

Cheese and Onion Rosti

You can make Rosti with just potatoes, potatoes and onion, or potatoes and cheese.

2 **potatoes**, grated

1 **onion**, grated

½ mug grated **cheese**

1 small **egg**, beaten

1 teaspoon **freeze-dried basil**

1 tablespoon **oil** to fry

salad to serve

£0.70 /PERSON

2

2

PREP 20 MINS

V

1. Squeeze the excess water from the potatoes and onion and mix with the cheese, egg and basil.

2. Divide into two and form 'cakes'.

3. Heat the oil in the frying pan and cook on a moderate heat for 5 minutes each side.

4. Serve with salad.

Chickpea and Chorizo Couscous

Couscous is so easy to cook, but you need to add plenty of flavour to it.

½ mug **couscous**

1 mug **boiling water** +
1 **vegetable stock cube**

½ teaspoon **paprika**

½ teaspoon **cumin**

½ teaspoon **ground coriander**

½ tablespoon **oil**

1 small **onion**, sliced

1 clove **garlic**, finely chopped

2 small **chorizo sausages**, chopped

400g can **chickpeas**, drained and rinsed

2 **tomatoes**, roughly chopped

¼ mug water

£0.65 /PERSON

2

2-3

PREP 10 MINS

1. Put the couscous in a bowl and add the boiling water, stock cube, paprika, cumin and coriander. Stir together. Cover with a plate and leave to stand for at least 5 minutes, until the water is absorbed.

2. Heat the oil in a frying pan or wok. Add the onions, garlic and chopped chorizo. Fry until the chorizo is browned.

3. Add the chickpeas, tomatoes and water, and cook for another 1–2 minutes, stirring frequently. Most of the liquid should be gone.

4. Add the couscous, mix together and serve.

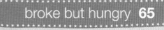

Tuna Hash

A good way to make one tin of tuna go a long way. Won't reheat too well, so make and share.

£0.95 /PERSON

2

2

PREP 25 MINS

2 medium **potatoes,** cut into 2cm cubes

2cm cube **butter**

1 tablespoon **oil** to fry

½ **red onion**, sliced

185g can **tuna**, drained of oil

½ x 340g can **sweetcorn**

1. Put the potatoes on to boil for 8–10 minutes, until they are tender. Drain and return to the pan. Add the butter and gently stir around.

2. Heat a little oil in a frying pan and fry the onions until they begin to brown

3. Add the potatoes, sweetcorn, and tuna to the pan and gently stir.

4. Heat on a medium heat and allow the hash to brown and then stir in the brown bits. Repeat twice. Don't keep stirring the hash or the tuna will go mushy.

5. Serve with mayo and crusty bread.

Big Wraps

This is the kind of recipe you can add and take away ingredients to suit your taste. There are enough tasty ingredients for you to leave out the meat if you are vegetarian.

£0.90 /PERSON

3

2-3

PREP 15 MINS

V OPTION

1 tablespoon **oil** to fry

1 **onion**, finely chopped

4 **mushrooms**, cut into fairly small pieces

1 **red, green or yellow pepper**, chopped

1 **chicken breast**, cut into small pieces

or 125g pack of **beef mince**

½ mug of **cooked rice** (see page 18)

1 small tin of **sweetcorn**

salt and **pepper**

4 **tortilla wraps**

½ mug of finely grated, strong **Cheddar cheese**

a few **cocktail sticks**

salsa (see page 137)

1. Heat a little oil in a frying pan and fry the onions 2–3 minutes until they begin to soften. Add the mushrooms and pepper and continue to cook for 2–3 minutes.

2. Add the meat and cook until it is no longer pink (leave out this step for vegetarian option).

3. Add the rice and the drained sweetcorn and cook for 2–3 minutes until everything is heated through. Season with salt and pepper. Take off the heat and leave in the pan to keep warm.

4. Gently warm the tortilla wraps under the grill, on low heat, for 2 minutes, or in the microwave for 10 seconds.

5. Place a wrap on a plate and put ¼ of the filling onto it. Sprinkle the grated cheese on the top. Fold the tortilla over and secure with a cocktail stick. If you don't have any, just roll the wrap over.

6. Serve with salsa.

Corn Fritters with Chilli Sauce

The dipping sauce is so easy and you can use it with other things, tortilla chips or patties, for example.

£0.90 /PERSON

4

(2-3)

PREP 20 MINS

V

4 tablespoons **flour**

2 **eggs**

½ x 340g tin **sweetcorn**, drained

2 **spring onions**, chopped

1 small **courgette**, diced quite small

½ x 200g block **feta cheese**, crumbled

salt and **pepper**

green salad and **dressing** to serve

Dipping Sauce

2 teaspoons **cornflour**

½ mug **water**

1 **fat red chilli**, deseeded and chopped

1 **spring onion**, finely chopped

2 tablespoons **wine vinegar**

2 tablespoons **tomato purée**

2 tablespoons **sugar**

1. To make the dipping sauce, mix the cornflour with the water in a small saucepan. Add the rest of the sauce ingredients, bring to the boil, stirring frequently. Turn down the heat and simmer for 1–2 minutes. Leave to cool.

2. To make the fritters, beat together the flour and eggs; it should be quite thick. Add the drained sweetcorn, spring onions, courgette and crumbled feta cheese. Season well.

3. Heat a little oil in a fry pan. Make the fritters by adding the mixture, about 1 tablespoon at a time, to the hot oil. Spread them out a little and fry on medium heat for 1–2 minutes each side. The fritters should be nicely browned and cooked through.

4. Serve with the chilli sauce.

one-pot dishes

Tired of washing up loads of pots and pans? These 'one-pot' dishes will minimise the clearing-up process.

Sausage and Bacon Casserole

Reheats well the next day, you can eat this with rice.

1 tablespoon **oil** to fry

6 large **sausages**

6 slices **streaky bacon**

1 **onion**, sliced

1 clove **garlic,** chopped finely

2 medium-sized **courgettes**, cut into bite-size chunks

400g **tin of chopped tomatoes**

1 tablespoon **tomato purée**

1 teaspoon **sugar**

1 **fat red chilli,** thinly sliced

1 tablespoon concentrated **chicken stock** + ½ mug water

400g tin **butter beans**, drained

crusty bread

£1.45 /PERSON

2

2-3

PREP 30 MINS

1. Heat a little oil in a wok, or large frying pan, and fry the sausages and bacon until both are browned. Remove from the pan and cut each sausage into 3. Cut the bacon into small pieces

2. Tip off any excess oil from the pan and fry the onions and garlic for 2–3 minutes.

3. Add the courgettes, tomatoes, tomato purée, sugar and chilli to the pan and cook for 3–4 minutes.

4. Return the sausages and bacon to the pan, add the stock, water, and the butter beans. Bring to the boil, season with pepper (the bacon will be salty enough). Turn down to simmer for 10 minutes.

5. Serve together with crusty bread.

Sausage with Apple and Mustard

This is a very simple, inexpensive 'all in one-pot' meal to make.

1 tablespoon **oil** to fry

4–6 **sausages**, pork, herby or vegetarian

1 small **onion**, sliced

2 medium **potatoes**, washed and cut into 2cm cubes

1 vegetable **stock cube,** dissolved in 1 mug of boiling **water**

1 **eating apple**, cut into chunks

1 teaspoon of **mustard**

2 tablespoons of **sweet chutney**

salt and **pepper**

£0.75 /PERSON

★ 2

2

PREP 15 MINS

COOK 15 MINS

V OPTION

1. Heat a little oil in a wok, or frying pan, and fry the sausages until they are browned on all sides. Take them from the pan.

2. Tip out any excess oil and fry the onions and potatoes, until they begin to brown.

3. Add the stock, water, apples, mustard, chutney and return the sausages to the wok. Bring everything to the boil and then turn down the heat and simmer for 10–15 minutes, until the potatoes are cooked. Stir a couple of times during the cooking process. Season well with salt and pepper and serve.

Sausage and Bean Casserole

If you are sharing a house with others, this is great if you double the quantity and share together. If you want to spice it up a little, add some curry paste or chilli flakes.

4 large **sausages**, pork, beef or vegetarian

1 tablespoon **oil** to fry

1 small **onion**, chopped

1 clove **garlic**, chopped finely

1 small **green pepper**, cut into slices

400g tin of **chopped tomatoes**

1 tablespoon **tomato purée**

1 tablespoon **Worcestershire sauce**

400g tin **baked beans**

baked **potatoes** or **rice** to serve (see pages 20 or 18)

1. Heat a little oil in a wok and fry the sausages. Take out of the pan and leave to one side.

2. Tip out any excess oil from the wok, fry the onions, garlic and peppers for 2–3 minutes.

3. Season well with salt and pepper.

4. Add the tinned tomatoes, tomato purée and the Worcestershire sauce. Cook for 5–6 minutes.

5. Cut each sausage into 4 and add to the pan along with the beans.

6. Serve with baked potatoes or rice (see pages 20 or 18).

Chilli Con Carne

Serve with rice, jacket potatoes, pasta or crusty bread. You can replace the baked beans with red kidney beans if you wish.

£1.00 /PERSON

2

2

PREP 20 MINS

V OPTION

1 tablespoon **oil** to fry

1 large **onion**, chopped

2 cloves **garlic**, finely chopped

250g pack of **mince, or Quorn**

400g **tin of chopped tomatoes**

1 **stock cube**, beef, lamb or vegetable

2 teaspoons **chilli powder**, more if you like it hot

400g tin **baked beans**

2 large **potatoes** to bake or **rice** to serve (see page 18)

1. Heat a little oil in a frying pan and fry the onion and garlic for 1 minute.

2. Add the mince and cook until the meat is no longer pink.

3. Add the tin of tomatoes, stock cube and chilli powder. Cook for 10 minutes.

4. Add the beans and cook for a further one minute. Taste to see if you would like more chilli powder. If you add more, cook for another minute.

5. Serve with rice (see page 18) or baked potatoes (see page 20).

Chicken Hot Pot

You can add other flavourings to the stock in stage 2. For example, 2 teaspoons curry paste or 1 teaspoon chilli paste.

1 chicken **stock cube**

1 mug hot **water**

4 **chicken thighs**, skins removed

3 **carrots**, washed and sliced

3 medium **potatoes**, washed and cut into chunks

2 sticks of **celery**, chopped

1 **onion**, cut into 6 wedges

2 cloves **garlic**, left whole

1 tablespoon **Worcestershire sauce**

salt and **pepper**

£1.50 /PERSON

⭐ **1**

🍴 **2**

🔪 **PREP** 5 MINS

COOK 75 MINS

1. Preheat oven to 190°C fan oven/220°C/Gas 7.

2. Put the stock cube in a mug, fill up with the hot water and stir until the cube has dissolved.

3. Put all the ingredients in a casserole dish. Season with salt and pepper.

4. Pour the stock into the casserole dish.

5. Cover with a lid or foil and cook for 1 hour 15 minutes.

6. You can take the lid off for the last half hour to let things brown a little.

Pancetta Risotto

Don't use margarine instead of the butter, the rice absorbs the flavour of the butter, whereas margarine has little taste.

£1.50 /PERSON

2

2

PREP 30 MINS

25g **butter** (measure by the packet)

1 **onion**, chopped

1 clove **garlic**, finely chopped

250g pack of **pancetta lardons**

1 mug **risotto rice**

2 **tomatoes**, chopped

2 mugs **water** + **vegetable stock cube**

1 mug frozen **broad beans**

pepper

½ mug grated **Parmesan cheese**

1. Melt the butter in a frying pan and fry the onions and garlic until they become soft.

2. Add the pancetta lardons and fry for one minute.

3. Add the rice, cook until the butter is absorbed into the rice.

4. Add the tomatoes, stock and water and season with pepper. The pancetta lardons will give enough saltiness.

5. Simmer for 10–12 minutes, stirring every now and then. You may need to add more liquid. Risottos should be creamy, not dry.

6. Add the broad beans and bring back to simmer for another 5 minutes.

7. Take off the heat and stir in the grated Parmesan.

Tuna and Lemon Pasta

Cooking the beans and the pasta in the same pan saves a bit of washing up. All together, a one-pot dish

£1.70 /PERSON

1

2

PREP 25 MINS

1 mug **pasta**

½ x 200g pack **green beans**

1 mug **frozen peas**

185g can **tuna**, drained

zest and juice of a **lemon**

2 **spring onions**, chopped

1 teaspoon **freeze-dried chives**

½ x 300g pot of **crème fraîche**

salt and **pepper**

a little **Parmesan**

1. Cook the pasta (see page 19). Add the green beans 5 minutes before the end of the cooking time and the peas 3 minutes before the end. Drain. Return to the pan.

2. Drain the oil from the tin of tuna. Add to the pan, along with the lemon juice and zest, spring onions, chives, crème fraîche and salt and pepper. Gently mix together, so as not to break up the tuna too much.

3. Serve with a little grated Parmesan over the top.

Spinach and Feta Frittata

Fritattas are very versatile, as you can add lots of different things.
They are also a good way of making a meal in only one pan.

100g **lardons** or **chopped streaky bacon**

1 tablespoon **olive oil**

350g can **sweetcorn**

200g **frozen spinach**, about 16 small pieces, defrosted and well drained

8 fresh **free-range eggs**

200g pack **feta**, cut into small cubes

½ x 250g pack of **cherry tomatoes**, halved

Dressing

juice of a **lime**

2 tablespoons olive **oil**

1 teaspoon **sugar**

salt and **pepper**

green leaf salad to serve

£1.50 /PERSON

2

4

PREP 30 MINS

---

1. Make the salad dressing and prepare the salad.
2. Heat a little oil in a frying pan and fry the lardons until they begin to brown.
3. Add the sweetcorn and spinach to the pan and cook for 1 minute.
4. Put the grill on to preheat.
5. Beat the eggs and pour into the pan. Cook. As the egg begins to set, gently move so the unset egg reaches the bottom of the pan.
6. While some of the egg is still runny, add the feta and tomatoes. Do not stir after this point. Total cooking time in the pan should be approximately 5 minutes.
7. Place the pan under the grill and cook until the egg is set and the top begins to brown. Should take between 5–10 minutes.
8. Cut into wedges and serve with salad.

Chicken Couscous

If you have leftovers, they are best eaten cold the next day and not reheated.

½ mug **couscous**

1 mug **boiling water** + 1 **chicken stock cube**

2 tablespoons **oil**

1 small **onion**, chopped

½ **red pepper**, chopped

1 **chicken breast**, cut into bite-sized pieces

1½ tablespoons **korma curry paste**

1 tablespoon **water**

⅓ mug **ready-to-eat apricots**, chopped

salt and **pepper**

1. Put the couscous, the boiling water and crumbled stock cube in a bowl and cover with a plate. Leave to stand for at least 5 minutes until the water is absorbed.

2. Heat the oil in a frying pan or wok. Add the onions and peppers and cook until the onions begin to soften.

3. Add the chicken breast and cook until no longer pink.

4. Add the korma paste, water and the apricots and cook for 30 seconds, stirring frequently.

5. Stir in the couscous, season well and serve.

Mediterranean Chicken

Sometimes, the skins on chicken thighs can produce a lot of fat. If so, just scoop off with a spoon before serving.

£1.80 /PERSON

PREP 15 MINS

COOK 50 MINS

4 **chicken thighs**

1 **onion**, cut into wedges

3 large **potatoes**, cut into 3cm cubes

1 clove **garlic**, finely chopped

3 **tomatoes**, cut into ¼'s

12 **olives**, chopped

1 teaspoon **freeze-dried basil**

2 tablespoons **olive oil**

salt and **pepper**

½ mug **water** + 1 **chicken stock cube**

paprika to sprinkle over

1. Preheat the oven to 180°C fan oven/200°C/Gas 6.

2. Put all the ingredients, except the stock and paprika, in a casserole dish. Distribute the oil evenly and arrange the pieces so that the skins of the chicken will brown. Add the stock and sprinkle the casserole with paprika.

3. Put in the oven for 45–50 minutes until the chicken is browned and cooked through. Test one piece to make sure.

something mum might cook

Missing home, never thought you would? Here are a few ideas to remind you of your mum's cooking.

something mum night cook

Roast Potatoes and Sausages

You can just use this recipe to make great roast potatoes.

1 tablespoon cooking **oil**

2–3 medium **potatoes**, each cut into 4

6 **sausages**, beef, pork or vegetarian

1 **onion**, cut into 6 wedges

salt and **pepper**

£0.80 /PERSON

1

2

PREP 5 MINS

COOK 50 MINS

V OPTION

1. Preheat the oven to 180°C fan oven/200°C/Gas 6.

2. Oil the casserole dish or baking tray and place the potatoes, sausages and onions in it. Distribute the oil over everything, using your hands. Season well with salt and pepper.

3. Put in the oven for 30 minutes. Take out of the oven and carefully turn things over, so that they brown on the other side. Cook for a further 20 minutes or until everything is browned.

4. Serve with baked beans.

Monday Pie

This dish is easy to prepare and will make enough for two meals. It is fine microwaved the next day.

1 tablespoon **oil** to fry

1 **onion**, sliced

½ x 500g pack of **beef, lamb or Quorn mince**

1 **stock cube**, beef, lamb or vegetable, according to mince used

400g tin **baked beans**

1 tablespoon **Worcestershire sauce**

4–5 **potatoes**, washed and cut into ½cm slices

£0.90 /PERSON

2

2

PREP 10 MINS

COOK 50 MINS

V OPTION

1. Preheat the oven to 180°C fan oven/200°C/Gas 6.

2. Heat a little oil in a frying pan and fry the onion for 1 minute.

3. Add the mince or Quorn and cook until the mince is no longer pink or the Quorn heated through.

4. Add crumbled stock cube, but no water. Stir well. The cube will dissolve in the meat mixture.

5. Add the tin of beans and Worcestershire sauce and pour into a casserole dish.

6. Place the sliced potatoes on top of the meat in layers and cook for 50 minutes. Test the potatoes with a fork to check that they are cooked. If not, turn the oven down to 160°C fan oven/180°C/Gas 4 and cook for another 10 minutes.

Lancashire Hot Pot

Bit of a lengthy cooking time, so plan ahead. Well worth the wait.

1 dessertspoon cooking **oil** to fry

2 **onions**, cut into 6 wedges, lengthways

3 cloves of **garlic**, finely chopped

250g pack of **cubed lamb**, you could use **lamb mince**

2 tablespoons **flour**

2 mugs **water**

1 **vegetable stock cube**

2 **carrots**

2–3 **potatoes**

salt and **pepper**

£1.45 /PERSON

2

2

PREP 10 MINS

COOK 90 MINS

1. Preheat the oven to 180°C fan oven/200°C/Gas 6.

2. Heat the oil in a frying pan and fry the onions and garlic until they brown slightly. Add the meat and cook until the outside is no longer pink.

3. Add the flour and stir well.

4. Add the water and the stock cube. Bring to the boil. The liquid should thicken.

5. Cut the carrots and potatoes into chunks and add to the mixture. Season with salt and pepper.

6. Transfer to a casserole dish with a lid and cook for 1½ hours. If you use lamb mince, you will only need to cook for 1 hour.

Quick Shepherd's Pie

This is an easy way to make Shepherd's Pie without the fuss of mashed potatoes.

250g pack of **lamb, beef, or Quorn mince**

½ mug **water**

1 dessertspoon **gravy granules**

6 medium **potatoes**, cut into 1.5cm cubes

2 teaspoons **butter**

salt and **pepper**

1 mug **grated cheese**

£1.30 /PERSON

2

2

PREP 20 MINS

COOK 25 MINS

V OPTION

1. Preheat oven to 180°C fan oven/200°C/Gas 6.

2. Put the mince into a pan with ½ mug water and bring to the boil. Simmer for 10–15 minutes. Add the gravy granules and stir. Season with salt and pepper.

3. Put the potatoes in a separate pan, with enough water to cover them, boil for 10 minutes and then drain. Add the butter and mix.

4. Pour the mince into the bottom of a casserole dish.

5. Carefully spoon the potatoes onto the top and sprinkle with the cheese.

6. Cook for 20–25 minutes until the top is browned.

Chicken Casserole

Quick and easy to prepare. Leave it in the oven whilst you relax.

1 tablespoon **oil** to fry

4 **chicken thighs**

1 **onion**, sliced

400g tin **chopped tomatoes**

2 cloves **garlic**, finely chopped

4–5 **mushrooms**, sliced

1 dessertspoon **Worcestershire sauce**

1 teaspoon **mixed herbs**

baked potatoes or **rice** to serve (see pages 20 or 18)

£1.50 /PERSON

2

2

PREP 10 MINS

COOK 60 MINS

1. Preheat oven to 180°C fan oven/200°C/Gas 6.

2. Fry the chicken until brown on both sides. Transfer into a casserole dish.

3. Fry the onions until soft.

4. Add the tin of tomatoes, garlic, mushrooms, Worcestershire sauce and herbs.

5. Bring to the boil and then transfer to the casserole. Put a lid on and bake for 1 hour.

6. Serve with rice or baked potatoes and green vegetables.

Roast Chicken

This recipe is for two to three people. If you just cook for yourself, use less vegetables and the leftover chicken can be used the next day, either in sandwiches, risotto or pasta dishes.

1 small **chicken**, approximately 1.5 Kg

4 large **potatoes**, cut into large pieces, see photo

2 **onions**, red or white, each cut into 6 wedges

oil

£1.45 /PERSON

2

2-3

PREP 5 MINS

COOK 105 MINS

1. Put oven on to 180°C fan oven/200°C/Gas 6.

2. Place the chicken in an oiled, flat, roasting dish or a casserole dish. Add the potatoes and the onion and brush with oil. Sprinkle a little salt over and, if you wish, add some rosemary. Cover with a lid or foil.

3. Cook for 1 hour. If you have a larger chicken, then cook for longer.

4. Take the lid or foil from the chicken and cook for a further 25–45 minutes, to allow everything to brown.

5. Serve with vegetables.

Parsnip Gratin and Sausages

If you cook the sausages in the oven, quite a lot of the fat will drain from them, making them slightly more healthy.

6–8 **sausages** (can use vegetarian sausages here)

2 medium **parsnips**, peeled and cut into chunks

3 medium **potatoes**, cut into chunks

1 small **onion**, sliced

100g pack **pine nuts**

½ mug **milk**

½ mug **double cream**

2 teaspoons **mustard**

½ teaspoon **nutmeg**

1 mug grated **cheese**

£2.25 /PERSON

2

2-3

PREP 20 MINS

COOK 30 MINS

V OPTION

1. Preheat oven to 180°C fan oven/200°C/Gas 6. Grease a casserole dish.

2. Put ½ a pan of water on to boil. Add the parsnips and potatoes and simmer for 10 minutes. Drain and put in the greased casserole dish.

3. Add the onions and pine nuts and mix together.

4. Put the sausages on a greased baking tray and put in the oven.

5. Mix together the milk, cream, mustard, and nutmeg in a bowl. Pour over the vegetables in the dish.

6. Sprinkle the cheese over the top and place in the oven for 25–30 minutes, until browned. The sausages should be nicely browned by the time the gratin is cooked.

Toad in the Hole with Onion Gravy

The secret of good Toad in the Hole is a hot oven and hot fat!

£0.55 /PERSON

3

2-3

PREP 20 MINS

COOK 25 MINS

V OPTION

Batter

1½ mugs **plain flour**

3 **eggs**, beaten

1 dessertspoon **wholegrain mustard** (optional)

pinch of **salt**

½ mug **milk** + ¾ mug **water**

2 x 2cm cubes **white Flora** or 2 tablespoons **oil**

6 fat **sausages,** pork or vegetarian

Onion Gravy

1 tablespoon **oil** to fry

1 **red** and 1 **white onion**, sliced

1 dessertspoon **flour**

1 beef/vegetarian **stock cube**

1 mug **water**

1. Preheat the oven to 220°C fan oven/240°C/Gas 9.

2. Put the flour in the bowl and add the eggs, mustard, salt and a little of the milk. Mix well, beating with a whisk or a large spoon. Add the milk and enough water to make the mixture look like single cream.

3. Put the oil or white Flora in a casserole dish. Place the sausages evenly apart in the dish. Place the dish in the oven for 5–7 minutes. The fat should be smoking a little after this time.

4. Pour the batter in; it should bubble around the edges as you pour it in.

5. Place the dish back in the oven, cook for 25 minutes or until browned. The mixture should rise around the edges.

6. While the toad is cooking, make the onion gravy. Heat the oil in a saucepan and add the onions. Fry for 5–6 minutes until they have softened and become quite brown.

7. Add the flour and stir well. Add the stock cube and the water. Bring to the boil. The gravy should thicken. Season well with salt and pepper.

Fisherman's Pie

Fish goes a bit rubbery when reheated, so this one is best shared.

£1.80 /PERSON

5 medium **potatoes**, washed and diced

2cm cube **butter**

2 pieces **cod** or **haddock fillet** (defrost if frozen)

1 mug **milk**

2 teaspoons **cornflour**

2 **hard-boiled eggs,** each cut into 4 (see page 26)

salt and **pepper**

1 mug grated **Cheddar cheese**

1 teaspoon freeze-dried **parsley** or **basil**

PREP 20 MINS

COOK 20 MINS

1. Preheat the oven to 200°C fan oven/240°C/Gas 7.

2. Boil the diced potatoes for 8–10 minutes, drain, add the butter and stir gently.

3. Place the milk and fish in the frying pan and simmer gently for approximately 5 minutes, or until the fish turns from opaque to white.

4. Mix the cornflour with a little milk and add to the pan. Stir into the milk, the sauce will thicken. Gently break up the fish and season with salt and pepper.

5. Add the hard-boiled eggs and the herbs. Mix together and pour into a casserole dish.

6. Place the potatoes on the top of the fish mixture and top with the grated cheese.

7. Cook for 20 minutes. The top should be browned.

8. Serve with green vegetables.

Corned Beef Bake

You could halve the quantities here, if you wish, and use the leftover corned beef in sandwiches. Is OK to reheat.

£1.10 /PERSON

3

3-4

PREP 20 MINS

COOK 25 MINS

2 mugs **pasta**

1 tablespoon **oil** to fry

1 **onion**, sliced

1 **courgette**, cut into small pieces

4 **tomatoes**, chopped

1 tablespoon **Worcestershire sauce**

340g tin **corned beef**, cut into cubes

1 mug grated **cheese**

1. Preheat the oven to 180°C fan oven/200°C/Gas 6. Grease a casserole dish.

2. Cook the pasta (see page 19). Drain and set to one side.

3. Heat a little oil in a frying pan and add the onions. Fry until the onions begin to soften.

4. Add the courgettes and cook until they begin to brown.

5. Add the chopped tomatoes and cook for 1 minute.

6. Take off the heat and stir in the pasta, Worcestershire sauce and corned beef. Season well with salt and pepper.

7. Pour into the casserole dish and sprinkle the cheese over the top. Put in the oven for 20–25 minutes until the cheese is browned.

Cheesy Potatoes

Cook the potatoes in a fairly large dish, so that there is more surface area to brown on the top.

2–3 **potatoes**, cut into ½cm slices

1 x quantity of **Quick Cheese Sauce** (see page 28)

1 extra mug grated **cheese**

salt and **pepper**

£1.50 /PERSON

2

1

PREP 10 MINS

COOK 35 MINS

V

1. Preheat oven to 180°C fan oven/200°C/Gas 6.
2. Arrange the sliced potatoes in layers in the bottom of the casserole dish.
3. Pour the cheese sauce over and season with salt and pepper.
4. Top with the grated cheese.
5. Bake in the oven for 30–35 minutes or until the potatoes are cooked and the cheese is browned. Test the potatoes with a fork. If they are not cooked, turn the oven down and leave for another 10 minutes.
6. Non-vegetarians can serve with bacon, sausages or salad.

Vegetarian

Searching for some interesting meat-free dishes? Treat your veggie friends to something special.

Vegetable Curry

You can add and take away vegetables from this recipe, depending what you have to hand. Make sure that the vegetables, which take longest to cook, go in at the beginning; carrots and potatoes, for example. Mushrooms, cauliflower and broccoli types need to go in towards the end.

£1.00 /PERSON

2

2-3

PREP 20 MINS

V

1 tablespoon **oil** to fry

1 **onion**, chopped

2 cloves **garlic**, chopped finely

1 **eating apple**, cut into medium chunks

1 **potato**, cubed

400g can **chick peas**

1 mug **water**

2 tablespoons **curry paste**, depending on taste

veg stock cube, crumbled

1 **courgette**, sliced

¼ mug **sultanas**

4 **mushrooms**, sliced

1 tablespoon **tomato purée**

Mint Raita

2 tablespoons **yogurt**, crème fraîche or soured cream

1 tablespoon **fresh mint** or 2 teaspoons freeze-dried mint

rice to serve (see page 18)

1. Heat the oil in a wok or frying pan and fry the onion until soft.

2. Add the garlic, apple, potatoes and chickpeas. Cook in the oil for 2–3 minutes.

3. Add the water, curry paste and stock cube, bring to the boil and then simmer for 10 minutes.

4. Add the courgette, sultanas, mushrooms and tomato purée. You may need to add a little more water. Cook for 5 minutes.

5. Serve with rice (see page 18).

6. To make the raita, just add the mint to the yogurt.

Vegetable Bake

You can use any mixture of vegetables for this dish. Make sure that there are some that you can fry at the beginning, as this gives more taste. Boil the vegetables which take longer to cook: carrots, potatoes, parsnips, etc.

£1.90 /PERSON

3

2-3

PREP 15 MINS

COOK 25 MINS

V

1 **carrot**, sliced

1 **sweet potato**, cut into chunks

1 small head of **broccoli**, broken into florets

½ mug frozen **peas**

1 dessertspoon **cooking oil**

1 **onion**, chopped

4 **mushrooms**, sliced

½ **red** or **green pepper**, sliced

1 **courgette**, sliced

2 teaspoons **HP sauce**

salt and **pepper**

double quantity of **Quick Cheese Sauce** (see page 28)

½ mug grated **cheese**

1. Preheat oven to 180°C fan oven/200°C/Gas 6.

2. Put the carrots and sweet potato into a pan of boiling water. Simmer for 5 minutes and add the broccoli and peas. Simmer for another 5 minutes. Drain well.

3. Heat a little oil in a frying pan and fry the onions until soft. Add the mushrooms, peppers and courgette. Cook for 2 minutes.

4. Mix all the vegetables together and place in a casserole dish. Sprinkle with the HP sauce and season well.

5. Make the Quick Cheese Sauce and pour over the vegetables.

6. Sprinkle the grated cheese over the top and bake in the oven for 20–25 minutes. The cheese should be browned on top.

Classic Nut Roast

You can use a variety of nuts in this recipe, but cashews, macadamians or Brazil nuts seem to work the best, as they have a slightly sweeter taste than some other nuts.

1 tablespoon **oil** to fry

1 small **onion**, chopped finely

2 **mushrooms**, chopped finely

200g pack **cashew nuts**, chopped

2 slices **wholemeal bread**

½ mug boiling **water** + ½ **vegetable stock cube**

1 teaspoon **Marmite**

1 teaspoon **mixed herbs**

£1.40 /PERSON

PREP 10 MINS

COOK 20 MINS

V

1. Preheat the oven to 180°C fan oven/200°C/Gas 6. Grease a small ovenproof dish.

2. Fry the onions in a little oil until they begin to brown, add the mushrooms and cook for a further 2–3 minutes. Take off the heat.

3. Add the chopped nuts to the pan.

4. Make the bread into breadcrumbs. Just rub it between your fingers; it does not matter if the breadcrumbs are a bit chunky. Add to the pan.

5. Add the teaspoon of Marmite to the stock and water and stir until dissolved.

6. Add to the pan along with the herbs. Mix everything together.

7. Pour into the dish and cook for 20 minutes. The nuts should be brown on top.

Cauliflower and Broccoli Cheese

If you are not a vegetarian, then you can serve this dish with crispy grilled bacon or sausages.

1 small **cauliflower**, broken into florets

1 small piece of **broccoli**, broken into florets

double quantity of **Quick Cheese Sauce** (see page 28)

½ mug grated **cheese**

1. Preheat oven to 200°C fan oven/220°C/Gas 7.
2. Boil the cauliflower and broccoli for 5–7 minutes (see page 16).
3. Make the Quick Cheese Sauce (see page 28).
4. Put the drained vegetables in a greased casserole dish and pour the sauce over them. Top with grated cheese and put in the oven for 10–15 minutes until browned on top.

£1.90 /PERSON

2

2

PREP 15 MINS

COOK 15 MINS

V

Pasta and Cheese Bake

You could add a teaspoon of Worcestershire sauce to the pasta, before adding the cheese sauce, if you are not a vegetarian.

1 x quantity of **Quick Cheese Sauce** (see page 28)

¾ mug **pasta**

1 **egg**, beaten

1 teaspoon **freeze-dried chives**

½ teaspoon **mustard**

2 **tomatoes**, each cut into 8

1 packet of **plain crisps**

½ mug grated **cheese**

£1.50 /PERSON

2

2

PREP 10 MINS

COOK 20 MINS

V

1. Make the Quick Cheese Sauce and leave to cool a little.

2. Preheat oven to 180°C fan oven/200°C/Gas 6.

3. Cook the pasta (see page 19).

4. Beat the egg in a mug, add the chives and the mustard and mix with the cheese sauce.

5. Put the drained pasta and the tomatoes into a casserole dish or oven proof bowl. Pour the sauce over the top.

6. Crush the crisps in the bag and mix with the grated cheese. Sprinkle on the top of the pasta.

7. Cook in the oven for 20 minutes. The cheese and the crisps should be browned.

Spicy Vegetable Pasta Bake

The vegetables can be varied. If you use things like potatoes and carrots, you will need to boil them before adding to the mixture.

1½ mugs **pasta**

1 tablespoon **oil** to fry

1 **onion**, chopped

2 cloves **garlic**, finely chopped

6 **mushrooms**, sliced

2 **courgettes**, sliced

½ **red** or **green pepper**, sliced

1 teaspoon **mixed herbs**

1 **red chilli**, chopped finely

1 tin Campbell's **condensed cream of tomato soup**, undiluted

½ mug grated **cheese**

salt and **pepper**

£1.75 /PERSON

2

2-3

PREP 15 MINS

COOK 25 MINS

V

1. Preheat oven to 200°C fan oven/220°C/Gas 7.
2. Cook the pasta (see page 19).
3. Heat a little oil in a frying pan and fry the onions and garlic until soft.
4. Add the mushrooms, courgettes, peppers, herbs and chilli. Cook for 2 minutes.
5. Add the tomato soup and bring to the boil and then take off the heat. Season well.
6. Drain the pasta and stir into the vegetable mixture.
7. Turn into a greased casserole dish and top with the grated cheese.
8. Cook for 25 minutes or until the cheese is browned.

Rice Salad

This is an ideal accompaniment to barbecues, or can be eaten with cold meats, sausages, baked potatoes, potato wedges or green salads.

1 mug **rice**

1 teaspoon **pilau rice seasoning**

2 **apples**, Golden Delicious or Granny Smith

2 tablespoons **olive oil**

juice of ½ **lemon**

3–4 **spring onions**, chopped

1 tablespoon **raisins**

1 teaspoon **freeze-dried chives**

250ml tin **sweetcorn**, drained

£1.05 /PERSON

2

4

PREP 15 MINS

V

1. Cook the rice with the pilau rice seasoning (see page 18).
2. Leave the rice to cool.
3. Chop the apple into small pieces.
4. Mix the oil, lemon juice and chives together.
5. Mix all the ingredients together. Serve.

Pasta Salad

Good for barbecues or with cold meats, sausages and other salads.

1 mug **pasta**

½ **red onion**, finely chopped

3 tablespoons **mayo**

1 **red pepper**, chopped

2 teaspoons **freeze-dried basil** or chives

2 sticks **celery**, finely sliced

salt and **pepper**

£0.30 /PERSON

⭐ **1**

🍴 **4**

🔪 PREP 15 MINS

V

1. Cook the pasta (see page 19). Drain and rinse under cold water.
2. Prepare the other ingredients and mix them all together with the pasta.
3. Season well.

Bean Salad

This is just a basic recipe. You can add other things to it, such as apples cut into small pieces, chopped avocado, or chopped fresh tomatoes. You can vary the beans, but it is best to mix 2 varieties. Always take care to rinse the beans well, as some of the soaking juices are not good for you.

2 x 400g tins of **beans**, flageolet, pinto, cannellini or haricot

½ **red onion** or 3 spring onions, chopped finely

1 **pepper**, chopped

2 tablespoons of **olive oil**

1 teaspoon **curry paste**

1 teaspoon **freeze-dried basil** or **chives**

1 teaspoon **sugar**

salt and **pepper**

£0.70 /PERSON

1

4

PREP 10 MINS

V

1. Wash and drain the beans.

2. Mix the pepper, onions and beans.

3. Heat the oil in a frying pan, add the curry paste and cook for 30 seconds. Allow to cool a little and then add the chives and sugar and add to the bean mixture. Stir and season well with salt and pepper.

Nutty Cheese Bake

Good one to make for your vegetarian friends when they come around.

1½ mugs **pasta**

25g **butter** (measure by the packet)

1 tablespoon **flour**

1 mug **milk**

150g **garlic and herb Philadelphia cheese**

½ teaspoon **paprika**

1 teaspoon **mixed herbs**

1 medium **onion**, sliced

100g pack of **pine nuts**

1 mug grated **Cheddar cheese**

£1.90 /PERSON

3

2-3

PREP 15 MINS

COOK 25 MINS

V

1. Preheat the oven to 180°C fan oven/200°C/Gas 6. Grease a casserole dish.

2. Cook the pasta (see page 19).

3. Heat the butter in a saucepan and add the flour. Stir well and cook for 30 seconds. Add the milk gradually and stir well. Bring to the boil, stirring frequently.

4. Add the Philadelphia to the sauce and mix until smooth. Add the paprika and herbs.

5. Heat a little oil in a frying pan and fry the onions and pine nuts until they begin to brown. Add to the cheese sauce.

6. Drain the pasta and stir in the cheese sauce mix. Pour into a casserole dish and sprinkle the Cheddar cheese over the top.

7. Place in the oven for 20–25 minutes until the cheese is browned on the top.

something for the weekend

Got a little more time on your hands and fancy something a bit different to eat? Treat yourself to something from this section.

something for the weekend

Mince Hot Pot

The potatoes need to be sliced thinly, or they will not cook in the allocated time.

1 tablespoon **oil** to fry

1 **onion**, chopped

250g packet of **lamb, beef or Quorn mince**

400g tin of **chopped tomatoes**

3–4 **mushrooms**, sliced

1 tablespoon **tomato purée**

1 teaspoon **freeze-dried basil**

1 **stock cube**, beef, lamb or vegetable

1 teaspoon **sugar**

4–5 thinly sliced **potatoes**

£1.50 /PERSON

2

2

PREP 15 MINS

COOK 50 MINS

V OPTION

1. Preheat the oven to 180°C fan oven/200°C/Gas 6.

2. Heat a little oil in a frying pan or wok and fry the onion for 1 minute.

3. Add the mince and cook until no longer pink.

4. Add the tomatoes, mushrooms, tomato purée, basil and stock cube and sugar. Bring to the boil and then transfer into a casserole dish.

5. Arrange the sliced, uncooked potatoes in layers on the top. Brush the top with oil; fingers will work if you don't have a pastry brush.

6. Cook for 45–50 minutes, the potatoes should be browned on top. Check that the potatoes are cooked, if not, turn down oven to 160°C fan oven/180°C/Gas 4 and cook for a further 10–15 minutes.

Spicy Coconut Chicken

Good meal to make and share. Will reheat well the next day or freeze.

£2.40 /PERSON

1 tablespoon **oil** to fry

6 **chicken thighs**

1 **onion**, sliced thinly

1 clove **garlic**, finely chopped

1 fat **green chilli**, deseeded and finely chopped

3 **tomatoes**, roughly chopped

1 teaspoon **turmeric**

1 teaspoon **ground cumin**

1 teaspoon **ground coriander**

juice of 1 **lime**

1 **chicken stock cube**

400ml can **coconut milk**

salt to season

rice to serve (see page 18)

⭐ 3

🍴 2-3

PREP 20 MINS

COOK 45 MINS

1. Preheat the oven to 180°C fan oven/200°C/Gas 6.

2. Heat the oil in a pan. Add the chicken and cook until the skin begins to brown, approximately 5 minutes. Remove from the pan and place in a casserole dish.

3. Add the onions, garlic and chillies to the pan and fry for 3–4 minutes until the onion is soft.

4. Add the tomatoes and the spices to the pan and cook for 3–4 minutes.

5. Add the lime juice, stock and coconut milk to the pan and bring to the boil. Season well. Once boiling, pour over the chicken in the casserole dish.

6. Put the casserole in the oven for 35–40 minutes.

7. 20 minutes before the end of the cooking time, put the rice on to cook (see page 18).

8. Take the casserole out of the oven and check for taste, season as necessary. Serve with the rice.

Bobotie

You can serve it with baked potatoes or salad. It is also great cold the next day. Best not to microwave, as it has eggs in it.

£0.70 /PERSON

2

2

PREP 15 MINS

COOK 40 MINS

1 tablespoon **oil** to fry

½ **onion**, chopped

1 clove **garlic**, finely chopped

250g pack of **minced beef**

2 teaspoons **curry paste**

½ an **eating apple**, unpeeled and cut into chunks

⅓ mug of **raisins**

1 dessertspoon **chutney**, Branston pickle or similar

1 **egg** + **milk** to make 1 mug of liquid

salt and **pepper**

1. Put the oven on to heat at 180°C fan oven/200°C/Gas 6.

2. Fry the onions and garlic in a frying pan for 1–2 minutes.

3. Add the mince and cook until the meat is no longer pink.

4. Add the curry paste, apple, raisins, chutney, salt and pepper. Stir well and heat through for about 2 minutes. Pour into a greased casserole dish.

5. Beat the egg in a mug and add the milk. Pour over the meat in the casserole dish.

6. Cook in the oven for 40 minutes, the egg mixture will set by then. Serve with jacket potatoes (see page 20) or salad.

Baked Chicken Topped with Cheese

You must use chicken breast, as legs and thighs will not cook in the time.

2 large **potatoes**

½ mug grated **cheese**

1 tablespoon **flour**

1 teaspoon **freeze-dried chives**

2 tablespoons **milk**

1 teaspoon **mustard**

2 **chicken breasts**

£1.80 /PERSON

2

2

PREP 15 MINS

COOK 60 MINS

1. Preheat the oven to 200°C fan oven/220°C/Gas 7.

2. Put the potatoes on to bake (see page 20).

3. Mix together the grated cheese, flour and chives. Add the milk and mustard and mix again.

4. Pile the cheese mix on top of the chicken breasts. Place on a greased baking tray or the bottom of a casserole dish. Leave until the potatoes have 30 minutes left to cook.

5. Bake in the oven, with the potatoes, for 25–30 minutes. The cheese should be browned.

6. Serve with salad.

Pasta and Chicken Bake

Take care not to over bake this, as the chicken will go dry.

£2.40/PERSON

★2

2

PREP 15 MINS

COOK 30 MINS

1 mug **pasta**

1 tablespoon **oil** to fry

1 **red onion**, finely chopped

4 small **mushrooms**, sliced

250g packet of low fat **cream cheese with garlic and herbs**

2 **chicken breasts**, cut into large slices

¼ mug **raisins**

1 tablespoon **lemon juice**

½ mug of grated **Cheddar cheese** or 200g ball mozzarella

salt and **pepper**

1. Preheat the oven to 180ºC fan oven/200ºC/Gas 6.

2. Cook the pasta (see page 19). Drain well and return to the pan.

3. Heat a little oil in a frying pan and fry onions and mushrooms in the pan. Cook for 3–4 minutes until the onions are softened. Add to the pasta.

4. Break up the soft cheese with a fork and add to the pasta. The warmth of the pan will cause the cheese to melt slightly.

5. Add the chicken, raisins and lemon juice, season with salt and pepper and pour into a casserole dish. Sprinkle the grated mozzarella over the top. Bake in the oven for 25–30 minutes until golden brown.

Spicy Chicken Meatballs

This dish is a little more difficult, try it after you have gained a bit of experience in cooking. You need to use fresh chillies, as dried ones will not taste the same.

£1.45 /PERSON

5

2–3

PREP 25 MINS

Sweet and Sour Sauce

1 mug **water**

2 tablespoons **tomato purée**

3 tablespoons **sugar**

2 tablespoons **white wine vinegar**

1 tablespoon **soy sauce**

2 teaspoons **cornflour**

2 **chicken breasts**, chopped finely

2 **spring onions**, chopped finely

1 **small red chilli**, chopped finely

198g can **sweetcorn**, well drained

1 teaspoon **flour**

½ beaten **egg**

salt and **pepper**

1 tablespoon **oil** to fry

rice to serve (see page 18)

1. To make the sauce, put all ingredients into a saucepan and stir well to mix in the cornflour. Bring to the boil, stirring frequently. Take off the heat and leave to one side.

2. Put the rice on to cook (see page 18).

3. To make the meatballs, mix together the chopped chicken, spring onions, chilli, sweetcorn, flour, egg, salt and pepper in a dish or bowl.

4. Heat the oil in the frying pan and put in dessertspoons of the mixture. Keep the heat at a medium level for 5–10 minutes. Turn the balls frequently, two forks will be the best tools for this.

5. Check to see if they are cooked by cutting through one of the meatballs. If the meat is no longer pink, then they are ready.

6. Reheat the sauce and serve with the rice.

Rainbow Trout with Thai Sauce

Easy way to cook fish, without it filling your house with unwanted smells for the next week.

£3.20 /PERSON

2

2

PREP 35 MINS

Sauce

1 teaspoon **freeze-dried coriander**

juice of ½ **lemon**

1 dessertspoon **honey**

1 tablespoon **oil**

1 teaspoon **fresh ginger,** grated

1 tablespoon **soy sauce**

2–4 **trout fillets** or 2 small whole trout

1 mug **rice**

½ teaspoon **pilau rice seasoning**

2 mugs **water**

½ x 250g pack **mangetout**

1. Preheat the oven to 180°C fan oven/200°C/Gas 6.

2. Mix the sauce ingredients together.

3. Prepare a piece of foil, large enough to wrap the fish, and place on a baking tray. Put the fish on the foil and pour the sauce over. Season with salt and pepper. Seal the parcels, pinching the edges together. Place in the oven for 15 minutes.

4. Cook the rice (see page 18).

5. Once the rice is cooked, thinly slice the mangetout and place on top of the rice. Leave the rice with the lid on, but off the heat, until the fish is cooked. The heat from the rice will cook the mangetout.

6. Serve the fish with the rice, spooning the juices from the parcels over the fish.

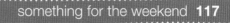

Fishy Pasta Bake

You can sometimes buy packs of fish pieces, either fresh or frozen, at a good price in the supermarkets. They are excellent for this recipe.

1 mug **pasta**

1 small stem **broccoli**, broken into 'small trees'

2–3 pieces of **cod fillet** (you can buy packets of frozen fillets)

1 mug **milk**

2 teaspoons **cornflour**

2 **spring onions**, chopped

1 mug **frozen peas**

1 teaspoon **freeze-dried parsley**

salt and **pepper**

½ mug grated **cheese** for the top

£1.50 /PERSON

3

2

PREP 20 MINS

COOK 20 MINS

1. Preheat oven to 180°C fan oven/200°C/Gas 6.

2. Cook the pasta and broccoli in the same pan for approximately 5 minutes, depending on the pasta you use (see page 19).

3. Place the (defrosted) fish and the milk in a frying pan and cook gently for 4–5 minutes. Remove the fish.

4. Mix the cornflower with a little milk and add to the hot milk in the pan. It should thicken.

5. Break up the fish gently and add to the thickened milk.

6. Drain the pasta and broccoli. Add to the fish mixture. Add the chopped spring onions, peas and parsley. Season with salt and pepper and stir gently.

7. Pour into a casserole dish and top with the grated cheese. Cook for 20 minutes. The cheese should be browned.

Bacon and Mushroom Pasta Bake

You can usually find pancetta lardons in the 'cooked meats' section at the supermarket. They are about the same price as bacon lardons, but much nicer.

1 mug **pasta**

200g **pancetta** or bacon lardons

6–8 **mushrooms**, sliced

1 **small onion**, chopped

150ml or ½ mug **double cream**

¾ mug grated **Cheddar cheese**

pepper

£1.40 /PERSON

1

2–3

PREP 15 MINS

COOK 25 MINS

1. Preheat the oven to 180°C fan oven/200°C/Gas 6.

2. Cook the pasta (see page 19). Drain well and return to the pan.

3. While the pasta is cooking, heat a little oil in a wok and fry the onions until they become soft. Add the bacon or pancetta lardons and cook until they begin to turn brown. Add the mushrooms and cook for 1 minute. Take off the heat.

4. Stir in the drained pasta and the cream. Season with pepper, the bacon will provide enough salt.

5. Pour the mix into a casserole dish and sprinkle the grated cheese evenly over the top. Place in the oven for 20–25 minutes, until the cheese is browned.

Bacon and Potato Bake

Make sure you cut the potatoes thinly or they will not cook in the allocated time.

1 tablespoon **oil** to fry

6 rashers of **streaky bacon**

1 **onion**, thinly sliced

3 medium **potatoes**, thinly sliced

2 **tomatoes**, chopped

½ mug **cream** or **milk**

1 mug grated **cheese**

pepper to season

£1.60 /PERSON

2

2

PREP 20 MINS

COOK 45 MINS

1. Preheat the oven to 160°C fan oven/180°C/Gas 4.
2. Heat a little oil in a frying pan and cook the bacon until it is crispy. Remove from the pan and cut into 2–3cm pieces.
3. Add the onions to the pan and cook until they begin to brown.
4. Layer the potatoes, onions, tomatoes and bacon in a casserole dish. Season with pepper.
5. Pour over the milk or cream and sprinkle the cheese over the top.
6. Place in the oven and cook for 45–50 minutes until the cheese is browned and the potatoes are cooked.

Oven Baked Risotto

You can replace the bacon lardons with pancetta lardons if you wish.

£1.35 /PERSON

2

2-3

PREP 20 MINS

COOK 20 MINS

1 dessertspoon **oil**

1 **onion**, chopped

250g pack of **bacon lardons**

1 mug **basmati** or **risotto rice**

4 pieces of **frozen spinach**, defrosted

2 mugs **water** + 1 **chicken stock cube**

1 teaspoon **freeze-dried basil**

3 **tomatoes**, chopped

½ mug grated **Parmesan cheese**

pepper

1. Preheat the oven to 200°C fan oven/220°C/Gas 7.

2. Grease a 20cm x 20cm casserole dish.

3. Heat the oil in a frying pan and add the onions and bacon lardons. Fry until the bacon begins to brown.

4. Add the rice and allow it to absorb the oil in the pan. Season well with pepper, the bacon will give enough saltiness.

5. Squeeze the moisture out of the spinach and add to the pan with the water, stock cube, basil and tomatoes. Stir together and bring to the boil.

6. Pour into the casserole dish and cover with a lid or foil. Place in the oven for 20 minutes or until the rice is tender.

7. Take out of the oven and stir in the Parmesan cheese.

friends around

Want to impress your friends, but not sure how? Here is something for when there is a hungry crowd to feed.

friends around

Pancakes

Pancakes are easy to make and are good fun when you have friends around. Just make sure you are not the only one standing cooking them! Tossing them is always fun, catching them not guaranteed!

2 **eggs**

6 tablespoons **plain flour**

milk

Trex or white Flora to fry (you can use oil but a lard type is best)

£0.20 /PERSON

2

2-3

PREP 20 MINS

V

---

1. Beat the eggs and flour together in a bowl or jug. Gradually add the milk, making sure there are no lumps. The mixture should be as thin as single cream, i.e. quite thin, but not as thin as milk.

2. Heat about 2cm cube of white Flora in a frying pan. When the fat begins to smoke a little, pour approximately 2 tablespoons of the mixture into the pan. Tip the pan around so that the mixture spreads over the surface of the pan. Let the mixture cook for about 1 minute.

3. Gently lift the edge of the pancake to see if it is browned. Once browned, turn the pancake with a slotted turner, or toss and then cook the other side.

4. Serve with lemon juice and sugar, undiluted squashes, any kind of ice cream, maple syrup, golden syrup, fruit such as strawberries, jam or ice cream.

Beef in Ale with Cheddar & Mustard Mash

When mashing potatoes, don't beat to a pulp, as they go 'glutenous'. Just mash until they hold together.

£2.10 /PERSON

3

6

PREP 20 MINS

COOK 90 MINS

1 tablespoon **oil** to fry

2 **onions** cut into wedges

1 kg **stewing beef**, cut into bite-size pieces

2 tablespoons **flour**

500ml bottle of **fruity ale**

2 tablespoons liquid **beef stock** or 2 beef stock cubes

salt and **pepper**

Mash

10 medium **potatoes**

25g **butter** (measure by the packet)

1 mug grated **Cheddar cheese**

1 tablespoon **wholegrain mustard**

12 **carrots**

2cm cube **butter** to cook

1. Preheat the oven to 180°C fan oven/200°C/Gas 6.

2. In a large pan or wok, fry the onions in a little oil until they begin to brown. Add the meat to the pan. You may need a little more oil at this point. Cook until the meat is no longer red. Stir frequently.

3. Add the flour and stir well to distribute evenly. Add the ale and the stock. Season well with salt and pepper Stir well and bring to the boil. The sauce should thicken slightly, but will thicken more as it cooks. Transfer to a casserole dish and put a lid or foil on to cover. Cook in the oven for 1½ hours. After 1 hour, give it a stir to make sure it is not sticking to the bottom of the dish. Add a little more water if the sauce is getting too thick.

4. About 35 minutes before the end of the cooking time, prepare the carrots. Peel and cut lengthways in half. Put in an ovenproof dish and add 2cm cube of butter and ½ mug water, together with plenty of salt and pepper. Cover the dish with some foil and bake in the oven for about 30 minutes.

5. While the carrots are cooking, put the water on to boil for the mash. Peel the potatoes, then cut them into 5cm chunks. Put them in the boiling water, bring back to the boil, turn down to simmer for 10–15 minutes until tender. Drain and return to the pan. Add the butter, cheese and mustard and mash. Leave with the lid on until needed.

6. Serve the Beef in Ale with the mash and carrots.

Chunky Chicken with Apples and Cider

If you want to use normal onions rather than spring onions, fry them in the oil before you add the chicken pieces.

£1.85 /PERSON

1

2-3

PREP 25 MINS

1 mug **rice**

2 mugs **water**

1 tablespoon **oil** to fry

2 **chicken breasts**, cut into bite-size chunks

4 **spring onions**, chopped

2 large **red apples**, cored and cut into small chunks

1½ mugs **cider**

½ **stock cube**

½ mug **cream**

1 teaspoon **freeze-dried basil**

1. Put the rice on to cook (see page 18).

2. While the rice is cooking, heat the oil in a frying pan. Add the chicken pieces and fry for 1–2 minutes, until they are no longer pink. Add the spring onions and apple, cook for 1 minute. Add the cider and stock. Keep on a high heat to reduce the cider, this may take 5 minutes.

3. Add the cream and basil. Bring to the boil and take off the heat straight away. Using fresh basil is best but not essential.

4. Serve with the rice.

Spicy Lamb Casserole with Mash

Lamb is a bit more pricey, but makes a good treat when friends are around.

£2.40 /PERSON

2

6

PREP 20 MINS

COOK 90 MINS

1 tablespoon **oil** to fry

2 **onions**, sliced

1 clove **garlic**, finely chopped

750g **stewing lamb**, cut into cubes

2 x 400g tins **chopped tomatoes**

1 **fat red chilli**, chopped

400g **chickpeas**, drained

1 tablespoon **ground coriander**

1 tablespoon **tomato purée**

1 teaspoon **sugar**

salt and **pepper**

6 medium **potatoes**

butter

green veg

1. Preheat the oven to 180°C fan oven/200°C/Gas 6.

2. Heat the oil in a large pan. Fry the onions and garlic for 3–4 minutes, until the onions begin to soften.

3. Add the lamb and cook until the meat is no longer pink and beginning to brown.

4. Add the rest of the ingredients and bring to the boil. Season with salt and pepper.

5. Transfer the contents of the pan to a casserole dish and place in the oven for 1½–2 hours. Stir a couple of times.

6. When the casserole is 20 minutes from the end of the cooking time, put the potatoes on to boil. Once tender, drain and mash with a little butter.

7. Serve the casserole with the mash and green veg.

Meatloaf with Baked Potatoes and Salad

You do need a loaf tin for this recipe. The meat loaf can be prepared ahead of time, giving time to relax before your friends arrive.

1 kg **beef mince**

1 **onion**, finely chopped

1 **egg**, beaten

1 teaspoon **freeze-dried basil**

5 pieces **sun-dried tomatoes**, finely chopped

8 slices **streaky bacon**

salt and **pepper**

4–5 **baking potatoes**

Salad dressing

1 tablespoon **olive oil**

1 teaspoon **wholegrain mustard**

1 tablespoon **wine vinegar**

1 teaspoon **sugar**

salt and **pepper**

salad

1. Preheat the oven to 180°C fan oven/200°C/Gas 6.

2. Lightly grease and line a 1lb loaf tin with greaseproof paper. Lightly grease the paper and line the tin with the streaky bacon.

3. Mix the rest of the meatloaf ingredients together in a bowl. Season well with salt and pepper. Place in the loaf tin, making sure that the bacon stays on the outside. See photo.

4. Place in the oven for 75 minutes. Take out and leave to cool for at least 2 hours.

5. One hour before you plan to eat, make incisions in the tops of the potatoes and put in the oven to bake for 50–60 minutes, depending on size.

6. Mix the dressing ingredients together. Pour over the salad just before serving.

7. Once the loaf is cool, slice with a sharp knife, ready to serve with the potatoes and the salad.

Beefburgers

Beefburgers don't have to be unhealthy. Make them yourself from good quality mince.

250g pack of **beef mince**

1 **egg**, beaten

1 tablespoon **oil** to fry

2 flat **bread buns**

any combination of **lettuce**, **gherkin**, **tomatoes**, **cucumber**, etc.

mayo, **tomato sauce** or **mustard**

potatoes for wedges

£0.80 /PERSON

3

2

PREP 5 MINS

COOK 10 MINS

1. If you want to serve these burgers with potato wedges, begin cooking them first (see page 134).

2. Mix the mince and half the egg together. Season well with salt and pepper.

3. Divide the mixture into 2 and shape the burgers with your hands so they are about 2cm thick.

4. Heat a little oil in a frying pan. Add the burgers. Cook for 4–5 minutes, then carefully turn them over. Cook for a further 4–5 minutes.

5. Using a fork, check to see that the inside of the burger is cooked, i.e. that the meat is no longer pink. If not, turn down the heat and cook longer, turning the burgers.

6. Put the cooked burger into the bread bun, add salad and the sauces to your taste.

7. Serve with potato wedges.

Lasagna

Once you have mastered Spaghetti Bolognese and the Quick Cheese Sauce, try this recipe when you have a few friends around.

Bolognese Sauce

1 tablespoon **oil** to fry

1 **onion**, chopped

2 **cloves garlic**, crushed

500g pack of **minced beef**, **lamb** or **Quorn**

400g tin **chopped tomatoes**

2 tablespoon **tomato purée**

1 teaspoon **sugar**

1 **stock cube**

1 teaspoon **mixed herbs**

salt and **pepper**

250g packet of **lasagna strips**

Quick Cheese Sauce

2 mugs grated **cheese**

3 tablespoons **flour**

2 mugs **milk**

½ teaspoon **nutmeg**

3cm cube of **butter**

salt and **pepper**

1. Preheat the oven to 180°C fan oven/200°C/Gas 6.

2. Put the cheese, flour and nutmeg in a saucepan and mix well. Add the flour and stir well. Gently bring to the boil, stirring frequently. The sauce should thicken.

3. Make the Bolognese Sauce (see page 63).

4. Use an oblong casserole dish. If you only have a round one, you will need to break up the pasta strips to fit. Firstly, put a layer of Bolognese sauce on the bottom of the dish and cover with some lasagna strips, making sure they do not overlap. Next, put a layer of cheese sauce, then pasta strips, then the rest of the Bolognese sauce. Lay more pasta strips and then the rest of the cheese sauce. Finally, top with some grated cheese.

5. Cook for 25 minutes. Test the pasta with a fork to see if it is cooked through. If it is not, reduce the temperature of the oven to 160°C fan oven/180°C/Gas 4 and cook for another 5–10 minutes.

6. Serve with salad or garlic bread (see page 24).

Tortilla Wraps

Tortillas are traditionally Mexican, but have become so cosmopolitan because you can fill them with an innumerable variety of ingredients! This recipe includes a few suggestions for hot fillings.

£0.50 /PERSON

2

2-3

PREP 15 MINS

V OPTION

1 **chicken breast**, cut into strips

1 tablespoon **oil** to fry

1 **onion**, sliced thinly

1 **clove garlic**, finely chopped

1 **red or green pepper**, sliced thinly

4 **mushrooms**, sliced thinly

1 tablespoon **tomato purée**

4 tablespoons **water**

½ teaspoon **chilli flakes** or chilli powder, add more or less according to your taste.

4 **tortilla wraps**

1. Heat the oil in a frying pan and add the onions and garlic. Fry for 3–4 minutes. Add the chicken pieces and fry until no longer pink. Then add the peppers and the mushrooms. Instead of chicken, you could use lean steak cut into strips (approx 200g), tofu or Quorn.

2. Add the tomato purée, water and the chilli, stir well and cook for a further 2 minutes to allow the flavours to mix.

3. Divide among the 4 wraps.

Optional toppings include grated cheese, feta, refried beans (spread over tortilla before the rest of the filling), sour cream and salsa (see page 137).

Beef Tacos

Fun food, best served and eaten straight away. Prop the taco shells up against each other to keep them upright.

£1.40 /PERSON

3

4

PREP 30 MINS

1 tablespoon **oil** to fry

1 **onion**, chopped

2 **cloves garlic**, finely chopped

500g pack **beef mince**

3 teaspoons **chilli powder**

1 teaspoon **paprika**

400g can **red kidney beans**, rinsed and drained

2 tablespoons **tomato purée**

2 **tomatoes**, chopped

1 **beef stock cube** and ¼ mug **water**

salt and **pepper**

Salsa

5cm **cucumber**, cut into small cubes

2 **tomatoes**, chopped

1 small **red onion**, chopped

juice of ½ **lemon**

1 tablespoon **olive oil**

salt and **pepper**

½ teaspoon **paprika**

8 **taco shells**

2 **little gem lettuces**

soured cream

---

1. Preheat the oven to 180°C fan oven/200°C/Gas 6.

2. Make the beef filling. Heat the oil in a frying pan or wok, fry the onions and garlic, until the onions begin to soften. Add the meat and cook until no longer pink. Add the rest of the ingredients and simmer for 10 minutes.

3. Mix the salsa ingredients together and cut the lettuce into thin strips.

4. Meanwhile, put the taco shells in the oven for 5 minutes.

5. Serve the tacos shells with layers of beef, lettuce and salsa, with the soured cream on top.

Potato Wedges and Dips

This is excellent party, or video night food, easy to make, almost like mum's chips!

£0.44 /PERSON

2

1+

PREP 5 MINS

COOK 25 MINS

V

Wedges

2 medium **potatoes** per person

cooking oil

salt and **pepper**

Optional flavourings - simply mix with the oil before spreading overs wedges

crushed **garlic**

rosemary

paprika (don't use too much as it is very hot)

small quantities of **curry powder**

finely grated **cheese**

---

1. Preheat the oven to 200°C fan oven/220°C/Gas 7.

2. Cut the potatoes in half, length ways, cutting each half into approximately 6 pieces and producing thin 'wedges'.

3. Oil a baking tray. You can use a casserole dish if it is large enough. Put the potatoes on it. Sprinkle more oil over the potatoes. Using your hands, toss the potatoes in the oil, making sure that every piece of potato is covered in oil. Separate the wedges, leaving all the surfaces open to brown.

4. Season well with salt and pepper.

5. Cook for 25–30 minutes in the oven, until the potatoes are crisp and browned.

Dips

These can be used if you have a party. Use carrot sticks, celery sticks, spicy crisps or cheese straws, or the potato wedges on the opposite page.

Cheesy Mustard

£1.15 TOTAL

½ x 300g carton of **soured cream**

½ mug finely grated **cheese**

1 teaspoon of **wholegrain mustard**

Minty Yogurt

£0.50 TOTAL

⅓ x 500g pot **plain yogurt**

¼ **cucumber**, chopped

½ **onion**, finely chopped

1 teaspoon **freeze-dried mint**

Soured Cream and Onions

£0.80 TOTAL

½ x 300g carton **soured cream** or crème fraîche

2 cloves **garlic**, very finely chopped

2 **spring onions**, finely chopped

1 tablespoon of **lemon juice**

Spicy Tomato

£0.50 TOTAL

½ x 300g carton **crème fraîche**

2 teaspoons **tomato purée**

3–4 drops of **Tabasco sauce** or 2 teaspoons chilli sauce

1 teaspoon **sugar**

Lemony Cream

£0.95 /PERSON

1 small carton of plain yogurt

3 tablespoons mayonnaise

grated rind and juice of a lime

Cheese and Onion

£1.50 TOTAL

½ x 300g carton **soured cream**

5–6 spring **onions**, chopped

½ mug finely grated **cheese**

1 teaspoon of **freeze-dried chives**

salt and **pepper**

Cheese and Chilli

£1.10 TOTAL

½ x 300g pack of **cream cheese**

1 teaspoon **chilli sauce**. Add more chilli if you like it hot!

2 tablespoons **crème fraîche**

It's so easy..

....with each of these, just mix together and season with salt and pepper!

Nachos

Nachos are so quick to make and are excellent for parties or snacks while you are relaxing, watching a video, etc.

½ x 200g packet of **corn chips**,
plain or flavoured

1½ mugs of grated **cheese**

Dipping Salsa sauce
(see next page)

£1.20 /PERSON

1

2-3

PREP 3 MINS

COOK 2 MINS

V

1. Heat the oven to 220°C fan oven/240°C/Gas 9.
2. Pile the chips on an ovenproof plate.
3. Sprinkle the grated cheese on the top and cover the chips.
4. Place in the oven for 2–3 minutes only. The cheese only needs to melt, it does not need to brown.
5. Pour the salsa over the top, serve and eat immediately.

Salsa

If you are having a party, these will work out much cheaper than the bought variety. Salsa is good with tortilla chips, quesidillas, and big wraps. If you like your salsa really hot, then adjust the amount of chilli powder or chilli flakes.

Dipping Salsa £0.90 TOTAL

1 tablespoon **oil** to fry

1 **onion**, finely chopped

3 **cloves garlic**, finely chopped

400g tin of **chopped tomatoes**

½ tablespoon **tomato purée**

1 teaspoon **chilli flakes**

½ teaspoon **paprika**

1 teaspoon **sugar**

2 teaspoons **freeze-dried chives**

1. Heat a little oil in a saucepan and fry the onions and garlic in a pan until they begin to brown.

2. Add the tin of tomatoes and bring to the boil. Add the tomato purée, chilli, paprika and sugar. Simmer gently for 3–4 minutes. Add the chives.

Avocado Salsa £1.40 TOTAL

1 medium **avocado**, peeled and chopped into small pieces

1 medium **onion**, finely chopped

2 medium **tomatoes**, chopped into small pieces

½ teaspoon **chilli powder**

¼ teaspoon **paprika**

½ teaspoon **sugar**

1 teaspoon **lemon juice** (this stops the avocado from discolouring)

salt and **pepper**

Tomato and Onion Salsa £0.95 TOTAL

4 **tomatoes**, cut into small pieces

1 **green chilli pepper**, chopped finely

½ **onion**, chopped finely

1 teaspoon **sugar**

1 teaspoon **lemon juice**

salt and **pepper**

For Avocado Salsa and Tomato and Onion Salsa, simply prepare the ingredients and mix together.

Chicken Drumsticks and Potato Wedges

Look out for bargain offers in the supermarket and buy a big bag of drumsticks; they will always come in handy.

£1.20 /PERSON

2

2-3

PREP 10 MINS

COOK 40 MINS

1 teaspoon **mustard**

1 tablespoon **tomato sauce**

1 tablespoon **Worcestershire sauce**

salt and **pepper**

1 teaspoon **brown sugar**

6 **chicken legs**

3 medium **potatoes**

oil

1. Preheat oven to 180°C fan oven/200°C/Gas 6.

2. Mix together the mustard, tomato sauce, Worcestershire sauce, salt, pepper and sugar.

3. Baste (spread over with a spoon) the chicken legs with half the liquid.

4. Place on an oiled baking tray or casserole dish. Bake for 20 minutes. Baste legs with the rest of the liquid and bake for another 20 minutes.

5. While the drumsticks are cooking, cut the potatoes into wedges (see page 134), place on a baking tray and sprinkle with oil, salt and pepper. Bake in the oven for 25–30 minutes.

6. Serve.

Toastadas with Avocado Salsa

You can vary the different types of salsa you use (see page 137) and make the toastadas more or less spicy according to your taste.

2 **soft tortillas**

2 **onions**, sliced

1 **green chilli**, finely chopped

400g tin **chick peas**

1 tablespoon **tomato purée**

1 teaspoon **Tabasco sauce**

1 tablespoon **crème fraîche**

5 **tomatoes,** sliced

300g block **Cheddar cheese**

salt and **pepper**

Salsa

3 **tomatoes**, chopped

1 **green chilli**, finely chopped

1 **avocado**, peeled and cut into chunks

4 **spring onions**, sliced

juice of a **lemon**

2 tablespoons **olive oil**

salt and **pepper**

£1.50 /PERSON

3

4-5

PREP 25 MINS

COOK 10 MINS

V

1. Preheat the oven to 200°C fan oven/220°C/Gas 7.

2. Cut each tortilla into 8 wedges. Place on a non-stick baking tray.

3. Heat a little oil in a frying pan and fry the onions and chilli until the onions begin to brown. Add the chick peas, tomato purée and Tabasco sauce and heat through. Blitz with a hand-held blender, or mash with a potato masher or fork; it doesn't need to be really smooth. Add the crème fraîche, salt and pepper and taste.

4. Place a dessertspoon of this mixture on each wedge of tortilla. Top with the sliced tomatoes and the grated cheese.

5. Place in the oven for 8–10 minutes, until browned.

6. Mix the salsa ingredients together and serve with the toastadas.

Moussaka

This dish can be quite rich, so serving with the green salad is a good option. For those with good appetites, serve with baked potatoes.

£1.35 /PERSON

2

4

PREP 25 MINS

COOK 30 MINS

V OPTION

1 tablespoon **oil** to fry

1 large **onion**, sliced

1 **clove garlic**, finely chopped

500g pack of **lamb mince, or Quorn**

1 **vegetable stock cube**, crumbled

400g can **chopped tomatoes**

1 tablespoon **tomato purée**

salt and **pepper**

1 large **aubergine**

25g **butter**, measure by packet

1 tablespoon **flour**

1 mug **milk**

½ teaspoon **paprika**

green salad or **baked potato** (see page 20) to serve

1. Preheat the oven to 180ºC fan oven/200ºC/Gas 6.

2. Heat a little oil in a frying pan and fry the onions until they become soft. Add the garlic and the mince and fry until the mince is no longer pink. If you are having baked potatoes, put them in the oven now.

3. Add the stock cube, tomatoes and tomato purée, bring to the boil and then turn down to simmer for 10 minutes. Season well with salt and pepper and put in the bottom of a casserole dish.

4. Cut the aubergine into 1cm slices. Heat a little oil in a frying pan and fry the slices for 1 minute each side. Put them on top of the mince in the casserole.

5. Heat the butter in a small saucepan, add the flour and stir well. Gradually add the milk. Gently bring to the boil, stirring well. The sauce should thicken. Add the paprika and pour over the top of the aubergines.

6. Place in the oven for 25–30 minutes until the top is browned. Serve with the green salad or baked potatoes.

Chicken with Pesto Pasta

You can use the rest of the feta cheese in sandwiches or salads.

£2.30 /PERSON

2

2-3

PREP 30 MINS

1 mug **pasta**

1 tablespoon **oil** to fry

2 **chicken breasts**

1 **onion**, cut into thin wedges

½ **red pepper**, cut into thin strips

1 **garlic clove**, finely chopped

12 **black olives**, roughly chopped

200g pack **cherry tomatoes**, each cut in half

Dressing

1 tablespoon **olive oil**

1 tablespoon **green pesto**

juice of a **lemon**

½ teaspoon **sugar**

salt and **pepper**

½ x 200g pack of **feta cheese**

1. Mix together the dressing ingredients.

2. Cook the pasta (see page 19).

3. Heat a little oil in a frying pan and add the chicken breasts. Cook on a high heat for 2 minutes each side. Turn down the heat and cook, with the lid on, for a further 4 minutes each side, depending on the size of the chicken breast. Test by making a cut in the meat to see that it is no longer pink in the centre. Set aside.

4. Fry the onions, garlic and pepper for 2–3 minutes until soft. Add the olives and tomatoes to the pan and take off the heat. The heat in the pan will cook the tomatoes sufficiently.

5. Slice the chicken into fairly thin slices and add to the frying pan. Mix together and serve on top of the drained pasta.

6. Cut the feta into small cubes and place on top. Drizzle the dressing over.

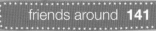

make your own takeaways

Tired of shelling out loads of dosh on takeaways? Make your own for a fraction of the price, plus you know exactly what's in it!

make your own takeaways

Sweet and Sour Chicken

You do need to use chicken breast in this recipe, as thighs and legs will not cook in the time.

£1.95 /PERSON

2

2

PREP 20 MINS

Sweet and Sour Sauce

2 tablespoons **tomato purée**

3 tablespoons **sugar**

2 tablespoons **white wine vinegar**

1 tablespoon **soy sauce**

1 dessertspoon **cornflour**

1 mug **water**

1 tablespoon **oil** to fry

1 **onion**, chopped

1 clove **garlic**, chopped finely

4 **mushrooms**, sliced

½ **red pepper**, sliced

2 **chicken breasts**, cut into pieces

227g tin **pineapple slices**, cut into pieces

rice to serve (see page 18)

1. Put the rice on to cook (see page 18).

2. To make the sauce, put all the sauce ingredients in a saucepan, mix together well, making sure the cornflour is evenly mixed. Heat gently and bring to the boil. The sauce should thicken. Take off the heat and leave to one side until needed.

3. Heat a little oil in a frying pan and fry the onion, garlic, mushrooms and pepper for 1 minute. Add the chicken pieces and cook until no longer pink, stirring frequently.

4. Add the sweet and sour sauce and the pineapple to the pan. Bring to the boil, turn down the heat and simmer for 3 minutes.

5. Serve with rice.

Chicken Curry

If you use chicken thighs in this recipe, precook them in the oven for 50 minutes in a casserole dish with a little water and salt and pepper.

£1.75 /PERSON

2

2

PREP 25 MINS

1 tablespoon **oil** to fry

1 **onion**, chopped

3 cloves **garlic**, finely chopped

1 **potato**, cut into 1.5cm cubes

2 **chicken breasts**

1 dessertspoon **flour**

¾ mug **water**

1 tablespoon **mild curry paste** (use less if the curry paste is hot)

1 **chicken stock cube**, crumbled

½ mug **natural yogurt**

rice to serve (see page 18)

1. Heat a little oil in a wok and fry the onion, garlic and potato.

2. Cut the chicken breasts into pieces and add to the pan. Cook for 2–3 minutes until the chicken is no longer pink on the outside.

3. Add the flour and stir well. Add the water, curry paste and stock cube, stir well.

4. Bring to the boil and then simmer for 10–15 minutes until the chicken and the vegetables are cooked.

5. Stir in the yogurt, but do not let it boil. Cook gently for 1 minute.

6. Serve with rice (see page 18).

Lemon Chicken

This dish is incredibly easy to make and tastes delicious. This recipe will cost a fraction of the price you would pay for a 'takeaway'.

£1.70 /PERSON

1

2

PREP 25 MINS

Sauce

1 dessertspoon **cornflour**

¾ mug cold **water**

juice of a **lemon**

3 dessertspoons **sugar**

2 whole **chicken breasts**

1 **lemon**, cut into slices

2 **spring onions**, cut into strips

1 tablespoon **oil** to fry

rice to serve (see page 18)

1. Put the rice on to cook (see page 18).

2. Mix the sauce ingredients together until smooth.

3. Heat a little oil in the frying pan. Add the whole chicken breasts. Cook on a high heat for 2 minutes each side. Turn the heat down to medium and cook, with the lid on, for a further 4 minutes each side. Check to see that the meat is cooked through; if so, remove from the pan and place on a serving dish.

4. Stir the sauce ingredients again and then add to the pan. Stir until the sauce comes to the boil. It should thicken. Add the slices of lemon and heat them over a gentle heat for 1 minute. Take off the heat.

5. Cut the chicken breasts into slices. Arrange the lemon slices on top and pour the sauce over.

6. Serve with rice and green vegetables.

Mini Pizzas

There are a variety of toppings here for you to try.

£1.50 /PERSON

2

4

PREP 20 MINS

V OPTION

Basic Tomato Sauce

1 tablespoon **oil** to fry

1 small **onion**, chopped

1 clove **garlic**, chopped finely

200g tin **chopped tomatoes**

1 tablespoon **tomato purée**

1 teaspoon **sugar**

1 teaspoon **freeze-dried mixed herbs**

salt and **pepper**

4 **muffins**

400g **mozzarella cheese** or 4 mugs grated **Cheddar**

Toppings

pepperoni or salami, sun-dried tomatoes, mushrooms and peppers

ham, pineapple and peppers

tuna and sweetcorn

sun-dried tomatoes and anchovies

sun-dried tomatoes, mushrooms and olives

red beans, mushrooms and peppers

---

1. To make the Basic Tomato Sauce, fry the onions and garlic in the oil, until the onions begin to brown. Add the tinned tomatoes, tomato purée and sugar. Bring to the boil and then simmer for 2–3 minutes. Add the herbs and the seasoning.

2. Put the grill on to heat up.

3. Cut the muffins in half, horizontally. Divide the tomato sauce between the muffins.

4. Arrange the various toppings on the muffins.

5. Grate the cheese and sprinkle liberally on top.

6. Using a slotted turner, transfer the muffins to the grill pan. Cook under the grill until the cheese begins to bubble and brown.

Chicken Noodles

This is nearly as quick as pot noodle, but much more nutritious and appetizing.

1 tablespoon **oil** to fry

one small **chicken breast**, cut into bite-size pieces

2 **spring onions**, sliced

¼ **red pepper**, chopped

½ **chicken stock cube**, dissolved in ½ mug boiling **water**

1 tablespoon **soy sauce**

150g pack of **straight-to-wok egg noodles**

salt and **pepper**

£1.90 /PERSON

2

1

PREP 10 MINS

1. Heat a little oil in a frying pan and fry the chicken until it is no longer pink.

2. Add the onion and pepper and fry for 1 minute.

3. Add the stock and the soy sauce together with the noodles and cook for 1 minute.

4. Serve.

Pork Noodle Stir-fry

It is best to use fresh egg noodles, but the ready-to-wok ones are fine. Cut the pork very thinly, fry quickly and it will stay tender.

£2.10 /PERSON

2

2-3

PREP 25 MINS

2 tablespoons **oil** to fry

2 medium-sized **pork fillets** or pork steaks, cut into thin slices

½ **red pepper**, thinly sliced

100g **mangetout**, cut in strips, lengthways

6 **spring onions**, sliced

2 **mushrooms**, sliced

200g pack of **fresh egg noodles**

Sauce

3 tablespoons **soy sauce**

2 tablespoons **rice wine** or **wine vinegar**

1 tablespoon **honey**

1 tablespoon freshly grated **ginger**

juice of a **lemon**

½ teaspoon **cornflour**

6 tablespoons **water**

1. Mix together the sauce ingredients. Set aside until needed.

2. Heat the oil in a wok and add the pork slices. Stir-fry for 3–4 minutes. Add the peppers, mangetout, onions and mushrooms. Cook for a further 2–3 minutes.

3. Add the sauce and bring to the boil, stirring frequently. The sauce should thicken.

4. Add the noodles and mix well. Heat through for approximately 1 minute.

5. Serve immediately.

Spicy Prawns

It is not recommended that you reheat prawns, so if you make enough for 2 people, it is best to share with a friend.

£2.00 /PERSON

2

2

PREP 15 MINS

1 mug **basmati rice**

2 mugs **water**

1 tablespoon **oil** to fry

½ **onion**, chopped finely

1 clove **garlic**, chopped very finely

200g tin of **chopped tomatoes**

1 dessertspoon **tomato purée**

1 teaspoon **sugar**

1 teaspoon **curry paste**

200g pack of **peeled prawns**, drained of water

¼ teaspoon **freeze-dried basil**

salt and **pepper**

1. Put the rice on to cook (see page 18).

2. Heat the oil in a frying pan and fry the onion and garlic in the oil, until the onions begin to brown.

3. Add the tinned tomatoes, tomato purée, sugar and curry paste and bring to the boil. Let the mixture cook for 2–3 minutes.

4. Add the prawns, basil and salt and pepper. Cook for 1–2 minutes. If you cook the prawns for too long, they will become rubbery.

5. Serve with the rice.

Chicken Teriyaki Stir-fry

You can use the other half of the bean sprouts in a stir-fry.

£1.80 /PERSON

2

2-3

PREP 20 MINS

rice to serve (see page 18)

1 tablespoon **oil** to fry

½ **onion**, sliced into thin wedges

1 **garlic** clove, finely chopped

1 **fat red chilli**, thinly sliced

½ **green pepper**, thinly sliced

2 **chicken breast**, cut into bite-size pieces

½ x 400g pack of **bean sprouts**

Sauce

6 tablespoons **teriyaki sauce**

2 teaspoons **sugar**

salt and **pepper**

1. Cook the rice (see page 18).

2. Prepare the ingredients for the stir-fry. Mix together the teriyaki sauce ingredients.

3. Put a little oil in a wok. Add the onions, garlic, chilli and peppers, Stir-fry on a high heat for 1 minute. Add the chicken and cook until no longer pink, stirring frequently.

4. Add the sauce to the wok and bring to the boil. Add the bean sprouts and stir-fry for 1 minute.

5. Serve the stir-fry on top of the rice, see photo.

comfort food

Want something to give you that warm, 'cosy' feeling, without spending too much money? Have yourself something wholesome.

comfort food

Mulligatawny Soup

If you reheat this soup the next day, make sure that it boils and then simmers slowly for about 3–4 minutes. Alternatively, reheat in a microwave for 2 minutes on a high setting.

1 dessertspoon **cooking oil**

½ **onion**, chopped

1 **carrot**, peeled and sliced

1 stick **celery**, cut into small pieces

1 eating **apple**, cut into chunks

2–3 teaspoons **curry paste** (mild)

1 **chicken breast**, cut into small pieces (leave out or replace with vegetarian substitute if vegetarian)

½ teaspoon **ground coriander**

3 mugs **water**

1 **chicken** or **vegetable stock cube**

400g tin of **chopped tomatoes**

¼ mug **long grain rice**

salt and **pepper**

£1.15 /PERSON

2-3

PREP 10 MINS

COOK 20 MINS

V OPTION

1. Fry the onion, carrot and celery.
2. Add the rest of the ingredients and bring to the boil. Simmer for 20 minutes, stirring occasionally.

Chicken Parcels with Mini Roasts

If you add other vegetables to this recipe, and they usually take a long time to cook, remember to cut them small.

£2.10 /PERSON

3 medium **potatoes**

1 tablespoon **oil** to fry

2 **chicken breasts**, left whole

10–12 **olives**

8 **cherry tomatoes**

3–4 pieces of **sun-dried tomatoes**, chopped

4 spring **onions**, chopped

juice of a **lemon**

1 teaspoon **freeze-dried basil**

salt and **pepper**

serve with **green vegetables**

PREP 10 MINS

COOK 25 MINS

1. Preheat the oven to 200°C fan oven/220°C/Gas 7.

2. Cut the potatoes into 2cm cubes and place on a baking tray. Sprinkle with salt and pepper, drizzle over some oil and then mix with your hands to distribute evenly. Place in the oven for 25–30 minutes or until browned.

3. Take a large, doubled sheet of aluminium foil. Place the chicken breast on the foil. Add the olives, cherry tomatoes, sun-dried tomatoes and the onions, distributing them evenly. Squeeze the lemon juice over, drizzle over a little oil and sprinkle over the chopped basil. Season well with salt and pepper.

4. Form the foil into a sealed parcel, just pinching the foil together where necessary and it will seal. Place the parcel on a baking tray and cook in the oven for 25 minutes. Carefully open the parcel, it will be full of very hot steam. Check that the chicken is cooked in the centre. If not cooked, return to the oven.

5. Serve with the potatoes, using the juices from the parcel as a sauce.

Vegetarian Spicy Soup and Herby Dumplings

You can use this dumpling recipe with other soups or in stews. Don't stir the soup too much or you will break up the dumplings.

1 tablespoon **oil** to fry

1 large **onion**, chopped

1 large **potato**, cut into pieces

1 large **carrot**, peeled and sliced

400g tin **chopped tomatoes**

1 **vegetable stock cube**

1 teaspoon **curry paste**, more if you like it hot

2 mugs **water**

3–4 **mushrooms**, sliced

Dumplings

1 mug **self-raising flour**, plain won't work, the dumplings will be solid.

½ mug **suet**

salt and **pepper**

1 teaspoon **coriander** or basil leaves (freeze-dried)

1 **egg** + **water** to mix up to ½ mug

1. Heat the oil in a large saucepan and fry the onions. Add potatoes and carrots and cook for 30 seconds.

2. Add the tin of tomatoes, stock cube, curry paste, water and mushrooms. Bring to the boil and leave to simmer gently while you make the dumplings.

3. In a bowl, a cereal bowl will do, mix together the flour, suet, salt, pepper and coriander.

4. In a mug, beat the egg and the water, add to the flour mixture and stir around.

5. Add just enough of the egg and water to form a soft ball of dough. Don't make it too wet.

6. Put some flour onto a board or plate and turn the mixture out onto it. Squeeze gently to form a ball, cut into 8 pieces, forming each one into a ball.

7. Add these to the simmering soup and cook gently for 10–15 minutes. If you have a lid, put it on the pan and the dumplings will cook quicker.

Beef Stew

Cooking the baking potatoes at the same time as the stew makes the meal simple and saves a bit of electricity/gas.

1 tablespoon **oil** to fry

1 **onion**, cut into chunks

1 **carrot**, peeled and sliced

350g **cubed stewing steak**

1 tablespoon **flour**

1 **beef stock cube**, dissolved in a mug of **hot water**

400g tin of **chopped tomatoes**

2 **baking potatoes**

£1.85 /PERSON

2

2

PREP 15 MINS

COOK 90 MINS

1. Preheat the oven to 180°C fan oven/200°C/Gas 6.

2. Heat a little oil in a pan and fry the onions and carrots until they begin to brown. Add the meat and cook until it is no longer pink.

3. Sprinkle the flour over the ingredients in the pan. Stir for one minute, making sure that the flour is evenly distributed.

4. Add the water and stock cube. Stir well, then add the tin of tomatoes. The sauce should thicken a little, but will thicken more as it cooks in the oven.

5. Place in a casserole dish, cover with a lid and place in the oven for 45 minutes.

6. After 45 minutes, put the baking potatoes in the oven and cook everything for a further hour.

Sausages and Cheddar Mash with Onion Gravy

You need to peel potatoes to get good mash. Mash does not need to be too smooth. If you mash the potatoes too much, they will become glutinous and sticky. The onion gravy can be used with other recipes.

£1.05 /PERSON

2

2

PREP 35 MINS

6 large **sausages**

4 medium **potatoes**

½ mug **Cheddar cheese**

2cm cube **butter** for the mash

Onion gravy

1 **onion**, sliced

2cm cube **butter**

1 dessertspoon **oil**

1 teaspoon **flour**

½ **beef stock cube**

1 mug **water**

salt and **pepper**

1. Preheat the oven to 200°C fan oven/220°C/Gas 7. Lightly grease a baking tray and place the sausages on it. Bake in the oven for 30 minutes.

2. Peel the potatoes and cut into 4cm chunks and add to the boiling water. Bring back to the boil and then turn down to simmer for 10–15 minutes until tender. Drain and return them to the pan. Add the butter and the cheese and mash with a potato masher or a large fork. Put the lid back on the pan and keep warm until the sausages are cooked.

3. While the potatoes are boiling, make the onion gravy. Heat the butter and oil in a saucepan, add the onion and fry until it is quite brown. You will need to stir frequently. Add the flour and stir until evenly distributed. Add 1 mug water + ½ beef stock cube. Stir well and bring to the boil. The gravy should be thickened slightly. Season well.

Bacon and Egg Bake

This is best shared on the day you cook it, as the eggs do not microwave well.

1 mug **pasta**

1 small head of **broccoli**, cut into trees

½ x 250g pack of **cherry tomatoes** halved, or 2 large tomatoes, chopped

½ x 300g **Philadelphia cream cheese**

1 mug grated **Cheddar cheese**

½ mug **milk**

1 teaspoon **mixed herbs**

salt and **pepper**

8 rashers of **streaky bacon**

2 or 3 **eggs**

£1.90 /PERSON

3

2-3

PREP 20 MINS

COOK 20 MINS

1. Preheat the oven to 200°C fan oven/220°C/Gas 7. Grease a medium-sized casserole dish.

2. Put the pasta on to cook (see page 19). Add the broccoli after 5 minutes. Cook for a further 5 minutes, drain and return to the pan. Add the tomatoes.

3. Mix together the cream cheese, half the grated Cheddar cheese and the milk. Heat very gently to melt the cream cheese. Add the herbs, season well with salt and pepper and pour into the pasta and broccoli.

4. Fry the bacon until it is crisp. Cut into bite-sized pieces and add to the pasta mix. Mix gently and pour into the casserole dish.

5. Make hollows in the pasta mix and break the eggs into them. Sprinkle the rest of the Cheddar cheese over the top.

6. Put in the oven and bake for 20 minutes.

Chilli Pie

Good video watching food. Be careful not to overcook the cheese topping, as the cheese still needs to be soft and stretchy.

2 tablespoons **oil**

2 **carrots**, peeled and chopped

1 **onion**, sliced

1 clove **garlic**

450g **minced beef** or **Quorn**

400g can **chopped tomatoes**

1 tablespoon **tomato purée**

1 **beef** or **vegetable stock cube**, crumbled

½ mug **water**

2 teaspoons **chilli powder**

½ x 225g bag **tortilla chips**

1 mug grated **cheese**

salt and **pepper**

1. Heat the oil in a wok or saucepan. Fry the carrots, onion and garlic until the onion begins to soften.

2. Add the minced beef and cook until no longer pink.

3. Add the tomatoes, tomato purée, stock cube, water and chilli powder. Season with salt and pepper and simmer gently for 15 minutes.

4. Preheat the oven to 200ºC fan oven/220ºC/Gas 7.

5. Pour the chilli mixture into a casserole dish. Place the tortilla chips on top and then sprinkle the cheese on top.

6. Place in the oven for 5 minutes until the cheese has softened.

date-night

Need to impress that special someone without slogging in the kitchen for hours? Try some of these 'scrummy' recipes.

date
night

Salmon Steak with Coconut Rice

Salmon is a little expensive, but wait for it to come on offer at the supermarket and buy in bulk and freeze some.

£2.30 /PERSON

2

2

PREP 35 MINS

2 **salmon steaks**

1 mug **rice**

400g tin **coconut milk**

1 teaspoon **freeze-dried coriander**

green beans

a little **oil** to fry

Sauce

2 tablespoons **mayo**

4 **anchovy fillets**, chopped

1 teaspoon **freeze-dried basil**

salt and **pepper**

---

1. Make the coconut milk up to 2 mugs of liquid by adding water. Bring to boil in the saucepan and add the rice and stir well. Bring back to the boil, turn down the heat and simmer, with a lid on for about 10 minutes, by which time the liquid should be absorbed.

2. Put the green beans on to cook for about 6–8 minutes, drain and return to the pan, with a lid on, until required.

3. While the rice is cooking, make the sauce by mixing the chopped anchovy fillets and basil with the mayo. Season well with salt and pepper and set aside.

4. Heat the oil in a frying pan. Add the salmon steaks and cook on a high heat for 2 minutes each side. If the steak is approximately 2–3cm thick, you will need to cook for a further 5 minutes on a low heat. With the point of a sharp knife, gently push the flesh of the fish apart to check that it is cooked through. For smaller steaks, reduce the time accordingly.

5. Stir the coriander into the coconut rice. Serve with the rice, green beans and the sauce.

Cajun Chicken with Potato Wedges and Salsa

Remember to keep your knife sharp, so that when you cut the chicken, you get good clean cuts.

£2.80 /PERSON

3

2

PREP 35 MINS

Salsa

1 medium **avocado**, cut into small pieces

½ x 340g tin **sweetcorn**

3 **tomatoes**, cut into small chunks

3 **spring onions**, chopped

1 **fat red chilli**, sliced into thin rings

1 tablespoon **oil**

juice of ½ **lemon**

1 teaspoon **sugar**

a few sprigs of **fresh coriander**, chopped finely

Potato Wedges

3–4 medium **potatoes**

1 tablespoon **oil**

salt and **pepper**

2 chicken **breasts**

2 tablespoons **Cajun chicken seasoning**

---

1. Make the salsa by mixing all the ingredients together.

2. Preheat the oven to 180°C fan oven/200°C/Gas 6.

3. Cut the potatoes into wedges and place on a baking sheet. Drizzle with the oil and season with salt and pepper. Mix with your hands to distribute the oil evenly. Stand the wedges up and apart from each other so they brown on all sides. Put in the oven for 25–30 minutes.

4. Put the Cajun seasoning on a plate. Press the chicken breasts into the seasoning and coat them well.

5. Heat a little oil in a frying pan, add the chicken breasts. Cook on a high heat for 2 minutes each side. Turn down the heat and cook with the lid on for a further 4 minutes each side, depending on the size of the chicken breast. Test by making a cut in the meat that it is no longer pink in the centre. Remove from the pan and slice (see photo).

6. Serve the chicken with the potato wedges and salsa.

Easy Beef Stroganoff

Bit of a 'treat' recipe, so very suitable for a date meal. Everything but the wine is essential in this dish for it to taste right. You can cook it beforehand, so you will only need to cook the rice when your date arrives.

£1.50 /PERSON

3

2

PREP 20 MINS

COOK 90 MINS

1 dessertspoon **oil**

1 **onion**, chopped

2 cloves **garlic**, finely chopped

250g pack of **cubed stewing beef** or beef cut into thin strips

1 tablespoon **flour**

1 mug **water** or one glass **white wine** (optional)

1 **beef stock cube**

1 dessertspoon **wholegrain mustard**

¼ teaspoon **paprika**

3–4 **mushrooms**

salt and **pepper**

1 mug **yogurt** or soured cream

2 teaspoons **freeze-dried basil** or parsley

rice to serve (see page 18)

1. Preheat the oven to 160°C fan oven/180°C/Gas 4.

2. Heat the oil in a frying pan and fry the onion and garlic for 1 minute.

3. Add the meat and cook on a medium heat until the meat is slightly browned, or until the meat is no longer pink.

4. Add the flour and stir well. Add the water (or wine + water to = 1 mug of liquid), stock cube, mustard, paprika and mushrooms and bring to the boil. Season well.

5. Place in a casserole dish with a lid (or use foil) and put in the oven for 1½ hours. Check every 30 minutes to see that the sauce is not sticking on the bottom of the pan.

6. Remove from the heat. Add the yogurt or soured cream and parsley.

7. Serve with rice (see page 18) and green vegetables (optional).

Mexican Beef

This is a little more expensive. You need to buy good quality beef steak, otherwise the meat will not be tender.

£1.85 /PERSON

2

2

PREP 15 MINS

1 tablespoon **oil** to fry

½ **onion**, sliced

1 **carrot**, cut into thin slices

1 clove **garlic**, finely chopped

½ **green** or **yellow pepper**, chopped

250g **rump steak** cut into thin strips

200g tin of **chopped tomatoes**

½ tablespoon **tomato purée**

½ teaspoon **chilli flakes**

salt and **pepper**

rice to serve (see page 18)

1. Heat a little oil in a frying pan and fry the onions, carrots and garlic for 2–3 minutes, stirring frequently. Add the pepper, cook for a further 2–3 minutes and then remove from the pan.

2. Add the thinly sliced beef to the pan and cook on a high heat for 2–3 minutes, stirring frequently until the meat is cooked.

3. Return the onions and pepper to the pan, add the tin of tomatoes, tomato purée and chilli and cook for 2-3 minutes. Season well.

4. Serve with rice (see page 18).

Tim's Special Mango Chicken

Mango pulp is a bit unusual, but is usually available at supermarkets. I can usually find it in Sainsbury's. If you cannot find it, simply buy a medium-sized mango, peel and slice it and mash it together with a little water.

£2.50 /PERSON

2

(2-3)

PREP 20 MINS

1 tablespoon **oil** to fry

2 **chicken breasts**, cut into bite-size pieces

4-5 **spring onions**, chopped

1 clove **garlic**, chopped finely

1 mug **mango pulp**

2 teaspoons **curry paste**

1 teaspoon **whole grain mustard**

1 tablespoon **soured cream**

rice to serve (see page 18)

1. Heat the oil in a frying pan and fry the chicken for 2 minutes, then add the onions and garlic. Fry for another 1 minute, stirring continuously.

2. Add the mango pulp, curry paste and mustard. Simmer for 2-3 minutes over a medium heat.

3. Take the pan off the heat and stir in the soured cream.

4. Serve with rice (see page 18) and vegetables.

cakes & cookies
Looking for some
comforting nibbles?
Try a few of these and
share them with friends.

cakes &
cookies

Rice Krispie Cakes

Mars bars do not melt as quickly as chocolate, so you need to be patient.

3 normal size **Mars bars** (58g) | 2 mugs of **Rice Krispies**
¼ x 250g block of **butter** | 12 paper **cake cases**

1. Cut the Mars bars into chunks.
2. Melt the butter slowly in a large pan and then add the chopped up Mars bars. Cook gently over a low heat, stirring frequently. The Mars bars will melt and form a thick, creamy mixture.
3. Add the Rice Krispies and stir quickly.
4. Divide the mixture into the 12 cake cases (use two spoons as the mixture will be quite hot).
5. It is best if you allow them to cool for 15 minutes, but one or two may disappear before then! If they last long enough, you can put them in the fridge.

£2.95 /TOTAL

1

12

PREP 10 MINS

COOL 15 MINS

V

Snickerdoodles

Leave the butter out of the fridge for a couple of hours to soften before you try to cream with the sugar.

½ x 250g block of **butter**, softened

½ mug **sugar**

1 **egg**, beaten

1 teaspoon **vanilla extract**

1⅔ mugs self-raising **flour**

½ teaspoon **nutmeg**

2 tablespoons **sugar**

1 tablespoon **cinnamon**

£1.70 /TOTAL

2

24

PREP 15 MINS

COOK 12 MINS

V

1. Preheat the oven to 160°C fan oven/180°C/Gas 4. Grease a flat baking tray.

2. Mix the butter and the ½ mug of sugar together and beat with a wooden spoon. Add the beaten egg and vanilla and beat well.

3. Mix in the flour and the nutmeg until the mixture is smooth.

4. Place the 2 tablespoons of sugar and the cinnamon on a plate and mix together.

5. Turn the cookie mixture out onto a surface and squash together. Make into a long sausage, handling as little as possible. Cut into 24. Take each piece and make into a small ball, roll this in the sugar and cinnamon, squash slightly and place on the baking tray.

6. Bake for 12 minutes. The snickerdoodles should be slightly browned.

Chocolate Chip Cookies

These cookies should be crunchy on the outside and a bit 'gooey' on the inside. Don't skimp on the butter and use margarine; it won't taste nearly as good! If you want to make double Chocolate Chip Cookies, then replace 2 tablespoons of the flour with 2 tablespoons of drinking chocolate.

½ x 250g packet of **butter** (make sure it has been out of the fridge for a while)

1 mug of **soft brown sugar**

1 large **egg**

1 teaspoon of **vanilla extract**

100g packet of **chocolate chips,** ½ milk and ½ white works well.

1½ mugs **self-raising flour**

£1.84 /TOTAL

2

16

PREP 15 MINS

COOK 12 MINS

V

1. Preheat the oven to 180°C fan oven/200°C/Gas 6. Grease 2 baking trays. If you only have one tray, you can cook them in two batches. The mixture will be OK to leave ½, while the other ½ cooks.

2. Mix the butter and sugar together and beat well. Add the egg and the vanilla extract. Beat well.

3. Add the chocolate chips and mix, then add the flour and mix well. The cookie dough will be quite stiff. Tip onto a floured surface and squash into a long sausage. Do not knead the dough. In fact, handle it as little as possible. Cut into 16 and roll each portion into a ball and then squash so it is about 1.5cm thick and approximately 6cm across. Place on the baking tray.

4. Put in the oven and bake for 10-12 minutes. The cookies don't need to brown, just be crisp on the outside. Leave a few minutes to cool.

Scotch Pancakes

You need to keep the pan quite hot for these, but not smoking hot!
To make sure they are cooking through in the middle, try one.

2 **eggs**

¼ mug **brown sugar**, can use white

I mug **self-raising flour**

¼ mug **water**

white Flora or oil to fry

1. Put the eggs, sugar and flour in a bowl and beat with a wooden spoon.

2. Add the water and beat well. The mixture is quite thick.

3. Heat a small amount of white Flora in a frying pan, until it is quite hot.

4. Put 4 separate dessertspoons of the mixture in the hot pan and leave to cook for 1-2 minutes. The mixture will rise slightly. Turn the pancakes over and cook on the other side for another 1-2 minutes. The pancakes will rise a little more.

5. Take out of the pan and eat immediately with butter and jam, maple syrup, ice cream, etc.

Flap Jacks

Makes good lunch time snacks, along with something a bit more healthy of course!

½ x 250g block of **butter**

3 rounded tablespoons **golden syrup**

½ mug soft **brown sugar**

2 mugs **rolled oats**

1. Preheat the oven to 170°C fan oven/190°C/Gas 4. Grease a baking tray and put a piece of greaseproof paper in the bottom.

2. Put the butter and the syrup and sugar in a large pan. Melt gently over a low heat. Do not allow it to boil.

3. Add the oats and mix well.

4. Pour into the baking tray, press down with a spoon and bake in the oven for 20-25 minutes.

5. Leave to cool for about 10 minutes. While the mixture is still warm, and in the baking tray, cut into squares. Should make about 18. Leave in the tin to cool and set.

£1.65 /PERSON

1

18

PREP 5 MINS

COOK 20 MINS

V

Nicole's Nutty Brownies

Brownies are meant to be soggy on the inside and crisp on the outside, so don't think they are not cooked, or that you have failed when you sample their delicious soggy centres!

½ x 250g block of **butter**

½ x 200g block of **dark cooking chocolate**

100g pack of **chopped mixed nuts**

1 mug of granulated **sugar**

½ mug **self-raising flour**

3 large **eggs**, beaten

£2.40 /TOTAL

3

15

PREP 15 MINS

COOK 30 MINS

V

1. Heat the oven to 160°C fan oven/180°C/Gas 4.

2. Grease a flat baking tray and line with greaseproof paper.

3. Put the butter and chocolate in a bowl, over a pan of simmering water, until they are melted.

4. Put all the dry ingredients into a bowl and mix.

5. Stir in the beaten eggs and then the chocolate and butter.

6. Pour into the baking tray and cook for 30 minutes. The brownies should be springy in the centre when you press lightly with your fingers.

7. Leave to cool. The brownies will rise in the oven and then go down when you take them out. Cut into squares when cool.

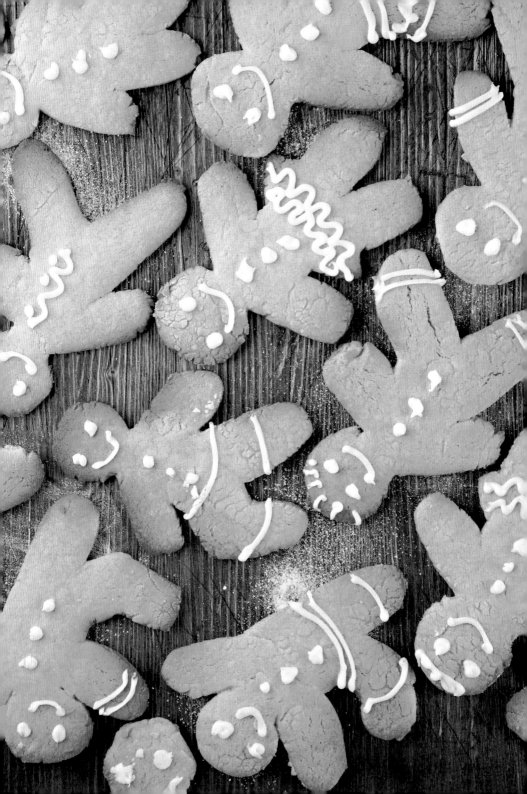

Gingerbread Men

You do NOT need a gingerbread man cutter, neither do you need to be an art student. Just draw your own gingerbread family on some paper, cut them out and then, when you have rolled out the dough, cut around them with a pointed knife.

If you do not have an icing bag, make one out of greaseproof paper. Take a square piece of greaseproof paper, make a cone and sellotape together. Put the icing inside and then snip off the tip of the cone. Screw the top of the cone around and squeeze. The icing should come out of the hole. Make sure the top end is screwed tight or the icing will come out of the wrong end!

£1.45 /TOTAL

4

12

PREP 40 MINS

COOK 8 MINS

V

100g or ⅖ x 250g block of **butter**

½ mug **sugar**

1 **egg**

2 tablespoons **golden syrup**

2½ mugs of **self-raising flour**

2 teaspoons **ground ginger**

icing

⅔ mug **icing sugar**

2 tablespoons **water**

1. Grease a baking tray with some butter.

2. Put the butter and sugar in a bowl and beat together with a wooden spoon.

3. Add the egg and beat well. Add the golden syrup and beat again until smooth.

4. Add the flour and ground ginger, mix together with a metal spoon. The mixture will be quite stiff. Turn out onto a floured surface and knead together. Cover with cling film and leave 1 hour in the fridge.

5. Put the oven on to heat at 180°C fan oven/200°C/Gas 6.

6. Place the dough on a floured surface and roll out. If you do not have a rolling pin, use a glass bottle. The dough should be about 1cm thick. Place the ginger people templates on the dough and cut out with a pointed knife. Squash together the spare pieces, re-roll and cut out some more men.

7. Place the men on the baking tray, cook for 8 minutes. If you only have one tray, the dough is fine to wait until each batch is cooked.

8. Decorate if you wish. To make the icing, simply mix together the icing sugar and water.

Muffins

Muffins are very easy and inexpensive to make. The flavourings can be varied according to what you may have in the cupboards.

3 mugs **self-raising flour**

1 mug of **brown or white sugar,**

2 **eggs**, slightly beaten

1½ mugs **milk**

¾ mug **vegetable oil**

Paper **cake or muffin cases**

£2.25 /TOTAL

2

24

PREP 10 MINS

COOK 20 MINS

V

1. Preheat oven to 180°C fan oven/200°C/Gas 6.

2. Mix all the dry ingredients together, then add the 'wet ones'. They will be a bit lumpy and quite 'wet'.

3. If you do not have the individual cake tins, arrange as many cake papers as you can on a flat baking tray. If you use them double, they will hold their shape better. If you only have one baking tray, the mixture will be OK if you leave it in the bowl whilst the first batch cooks. Bake in the oven for 20 minutes. If you use the larger muffin cases, you will need to bake them for 25 minutes.

Variations

Chocolate chip muffins

Add two 100g packets of chocolate chips. Two different varieties work well; for example, white and milk or plain chocolate. If you want double choc chip muffins, instead of the 3 mugs of flour, use 2⅔ flour and ⅓ mug drinking chocolate.

Raspberry or blueberry muffins

Take a 400g tin of the fruit, drain away the liquid and add the fruit with the wet ingredients.

Apple cinnamon muffins

Add 1 mug of finely chopped apple with the wet ingredients, and 2 teaspoons ground cinnamon to the dry ingredients.

Banana and nuts

Add 1 mug of mashed, ripe banana + 1 mug of chopped nuts, (cashews, Brazils, pecans or walnuts) along with the wet ingredients.

Scones

Scones are delicious with jam and cream, but you can make them with cheese and, depending on your taste, also eat them with jam, but not the cream! They are a fun Sunday afternoon snack.

Basic plain scones

2 mugs of **self-raising flour**

¼ teaspoon **salt**

½ x 250g block of **butter**

1 **egg**, beaten + **milk** to make ⅔ of a mug

Savoury

Add ¾ mug of **grated cheese** before you add the liquid.

Sweet

Add ⅓ mug of **sugar**. If you want, you can also add ½ mug of **raisins**.

1. Preheat the oven to 180ºC fan oven/200ºC/Gas 6. Grease a flat baking tray.

2. Place flour and salt in a bowl. Chop the butter into small pieces, add to the flour and rub in with your fingers. Try not to work it too much or for too long.

3. If you are making plain scones, go to pt. 4. If you are making either of the variations, add the extra ingredients in now and stir.

4. Add the egg and milk to the mixture and mix well with a knife. The mixture should be soft, but not sticky.

5. Turn out on to a floured surface and gently squash the mixture so it is flat and about 5cm thick. Do not knead at this point. The less you handle the mixture the better. Use round cutters if you have them, but if not, squash the mixture into a neat square shape and cut square scones, as in the photo.

6. Place them on the tray, with a little space between them for them to rise and spread. Brush the top of the scones with some milk. Use your fingers if you do not have a brush.

7. Place in the oven for 15-20 minutes. They should rise a little and be brown on the top. If they spread into one another, don't worry, allow them to cool and you will be able to pull them apart.

Choc Mint Slices

Add the water to the icing sugar gradually, as it can easily become too runny.

1½ x 300g packets of **hob nobs**
6 tablespoons **drinking chocolate**
250g block **butter**
2 mugs **icing sugar**

4 tablespoons **water**
2 teaspoons **peppermint essence**
200g block of **chocolate**

£3.95 /TOTAL

5

18

PREP 30 MINS

COOL 1 HOUR

V

1. Line an 18cm x 27cm baking tray with greaseproof paper.

2. Put the hob nobs in a plastic bag and bash with a rolling pin, or similar implement, until you have quite fine crumbs.

3. Stir in the drinking chocolate.

4. Gently melt the butter in a saucepan. Pour over the biscuits and mix well.

5. Pour into the tray and press down well. Leave in the fridge for 1 hour.

6. Mix together the icing sugar, peppermint essence and the water. The mixture should be very stiff. Spread over the chocolate biscuit base. Leave for 1 hour to set a little.

7. Gently melt the chocolate in a bowl over a pan of simmering water. Carefully spread the chocolate over the icing.

8. Leave in the fridge for 1 hour. When you cut into squares, heat the knife under the hot water tap and it will stop the chocolate from cracking too much.

Chocolate Fridge Slices

These would make really good presents if you put them in a little box or make a fabric bag and tie with some ribbon. Think this suggestion could be limited to the girls, but you guys can take up the challenge and have a go!

⅗ x 250g block **butter**

200g **white chocolate**

100g **dark chocolate**

300g pack of **hob nob biscuits**

1 teaspoon **vanilla extract**

250ml pot of **crème fraîche**

½ x 250g packet of **ready-to-eat apricots**, chopped

100g packet of **hazelnuts** or pistachios, chopped

£5.90 /TOTAL

2

20

PREP 30 MINS

COOL 3 HRS

V

1. Grease and line a 25cm x17cm baking tray tin.

2. Place the butter and the chocolate in a bowl. Put over a pan of gently boiling water and allow to melt. Stir every now and then.

3. While the chocolate is melting, put the biscuits in a plastic bag and gently bash them with a rolling pin or similar implement. Keep them fairly rustic, don't beat them to dust.

4. Once the chocolate has melted, take off the heat and add the vanilla and stir well.

5. Add the crème fraîche and stir until it has melted into the chocolate.

6. Add the apricots and nuts and stir.

7. Put the biscuit crumbs into a larger bowl and add the chocolate mixture to them. The mixture will still be quite runny. Pour into the baking tray and place in the fridge for a minimum of 3 hours, preferably overnight.

8. Tip out onto a chopping board, take the greaseproof off the bottom and cut into slices. This recipe is quite rich, so don't make the slices too big. Keep in the fridge until needed.

Chocolate Cake

If you regularly make cakes and cookies you might want to invest in some electric beaters. You can usually pick them up in the supermarket for about £12.00. This would make an excellent birthday cake for your friends.

⅓ x 500g tub of **soft margarine or butter**

¾ mug **sugar**

3 **eggs**

1 mug **self-raising flour**

3 tablespoons **drinking chocolate**

1 tablespoon **water** if required

Filling and topping

small carton of **cream** for the filling

140g bar of **Dairy Milk**

1 **Flake** for the topping

1. Preheat the oven to 180°C/fan/200°C/Gas 6.

2. Grease two 20cm round cake tins. Cut a round of greaseproof paper and put in the bottom of the cake tins.

3. Put the butter and sugar in a bowl. Beat well with a wooden spoon.

4. Add the eggs, one at a time, and beat well. The mixture should go quite pale.

5. Add the flour and drinking chocolate, fold in gently with a metal spoon. Do not beat the cake mixture at this stage. If the eggs used were small and the mixture is very stiff, add one tablespoon of water.

6. Pour the mixture into the tins and smooth out the top. Place in the oven for 25-30 minutes. When the cake is done, you should be able to gently press it in the centre and it will not leave an indentation, but rather 'bounce' back a little.

7. Leave the cake to cool.

8. Put one of the cakes up-side down on a plate and spread with fresh whipped cream. Put the other cake, right way up, on top.

9. Melt a bar of Dairy Milk in a bowl over a pan of simmering water. Spread it over the top of the cake. You can sprinkle a broken up Flake on top, in order to make the whole thing completely naughty!

Astri's Apple Cake

These cakes can also be used as a dessert, if you serve them with cream or custard.

2 medium-sized **apples** (cooking apples are best, but you can use eating apples)

150g or ⅗ x 250g block **butter**

¾ mug **sugar**

3 **eggs**

2 drops of **vanilla essence** (optional)

1½ mugs **self-raising flour**

3 tablespoons cold **water**

Topping

¼ mug **sugar**

1 teaspoon **cinnamon**

£2.45 /TOTAL

3

16

PREP 20 MINS

COOK 25 MINS

V

---

1. Preheat the oven to 180°C fan oven/200°C/Gas 6. Grease a baking tray and put a piece of greaseproof paper in the bottom of the tray.

2. Put the sugar and cinnamon in a mug and mix.

3. Peel the apples, cut into ¼'s, take out the core and slice each ¼ lengthways again 3 or 4 times, making thin slivers of apple. Set aside.

4. Cream the butter and sugar together with a wooden spoon until the mixture becomes soft and lightens in colour. Add the eggs and beat well. Add the vanilla essence.

5. Fold in the flour with a metal spoon. Do not beat. Add the water and stir gently. The mixture should still be quite stiff.

6. Turn into the baking tray and spread out evenly. Push the apple slices into the mix, distributing them as evenly as possible. Sprinkle the sugar and cinnamon evenly over the top.

7. Bake in the oven for 25 minutes. The top should be nicely brown.

8. Leave to cool and cut into slices.

desserts

Think that making desserts is too difficult, but you have some friends around? Try some of these, just don't think about the calories!

desserts

Quick Cheese Cake

In order to get the cheesecake out of the tin, you will need to use a cake tin with a loose bottom. It is best to put a circle of greaseproof paper in the bottom. Once the cheesecake has set, loosen the side with a knife and place the loose-bottomed tin on a jam jar or tin and push the sides down.

£3.45 /TOTAL

3

4

PREP 20 MINS

COOL 4 HRS

V

250g packet of **digestive biscuits** or **hob nobs**

¼ x 500g pack of **butter**

300ml pot of **double cream**

2 tablespoons **white sugar**

300g packet of **cream cheese**

rind and juice of a **lemon**

fruit to decorate, e.g. **oranges**, **raspberries** or **strawberries**

1. Put the digestive biscuits into a polythene bag and crush them with a rolling pin or similar implement (tin of beans). There should be no lumps left, just crumbs!

2. Melt the butter in a saucepan and add the crushed biscuit. Mix well.

3. Press the biscuit mixture into the bottom of a 20cm cake tin. If you do not have a cake tin, use a small casserole dish (don't try to get the cake out whole, just cut into pieces in the dish).

4. Beat the cream and sugar together with a whisk until the cream thickens. Don't keep beating once thickened, or it will turn to butter.

5. Gently fold in the cream cheese, grated lemon rind and juice. The lemon juice is essential, as it helps the cream to set. Pour on to the top of the biscuit mixture and gently spread out.

6. Leave in the fridge for 4 hours to set.

7. Decorate the top with fruit.

Ice Cream and Chocolate Sauce

This is a very quick and easy way of producing a dessert if you have friends around for a meal. Keep the sauce ingredients in your store cupboard and the ice cream in your freezer drawer! You can add things on top of the chocolate sauce, such as chopped nuts, 100's and 1000's, Smarties, broken up Flakes, small sweets, etc.

You will need to leave the sauce to cool longer, if you are using glass dishes, as the contrasts in temperature between the sauce and the ice cream may break thinner glass.

¼ x 500g pack **butter**

3 heaped tablespoons **drinking chocolate**

4 heaped tablespoons **sugar** (brown or white)

2 tablespoons **milk** or **cream**

ice cream

1. Place the butter, sugar and chocolate in a saucepan. Heat gently, stir well, and allow to simmer for 1 minute.

2. Add the milk or cream carefully, as it may spit at you! Simmer for another 1 minute, stirring all the time until smooth and thick.

3. Allow to cool slightly before serving on top of the ice cream.

Fruit Fool

As the cream begins to thicken, be careful and beat more slowly, so that it does not turn into butter.

500g **mascarpone cheese**
½ mug **double cream**, whipped
6 tablespoons **icing sugar**,
1 **lemon**, zest and juice

½ x 400g pack of **frozen summer fruits**, defrosted
1 small **white chocolate bar**, grated
amaretti biscuits (optional)

£1.55 /PERSON

2

4

PREP 15 MINS

COOL 2 HRS

V

1. Mix together the mascarpone and the whipped, double cream and sugar. Add the lemon zest and juice, mix well.

2. Add the fruits (retain a few for decoration). Stir them in, trying not to completely break them up.

3. Spoon into individual dishes and leave in the fridge for 2 hours.

4. To serve, decorate the dishes with grated white chocolate and fruits.

Fruit Salad

This will not really last more than one day, as the fruits will begin to go brown. You can use a variety of fruits chosen from the list below.

£1.30 /PERSON

1

2-3

PREP 15 MINS

V

apples

pears

oranges

bananas

seedless grapes

strawberries

kiwi fruits

pineapple

peaches

nectarines

raspberries

For the juice

You can use cartons of pure **apple** or **orange** **fruit juice**.

If you prefer a more tangy fruit juice, try the following:

1 **lemon**

1 **orange**

1 tablespoon **sugar**

¼ mug **water**

1. To make the tangy fruit juice, grate the rind of the lemon and the orange and squeeze the juices from both fruits. Add the sugar and the water. Leave for the sugar to dissolve.

2. Cut the fruit into small pieces and mix together. If you use raspberries and strawberries, add them at the end or they will break up in the mix and everything will be pink!

3. Serve with whipped cream.

Banana Split

Make just before you serve, as the bananas will go brown if left for a long time.

Chocolate Sauce (see page 192)   2 scoops of **ice cream**

1 **banana**   1 **Cadbury's Flake**

1. Make the Chocolate Sauce.
2. Slice the banana in half lengthways and arrange on the plate or dish.
3. Place 2 scoops of ice cream on the plate, pour the chocolate sauce over and sprinkle the broken-up flake over the top.

Other ideas for 'easy ice cream' type desserts:

Sundaes made from layers of different flavours of ice cream, mixed with fresh or tinned fruit, chocolate or jam sponge rolls. You can decorate them with many varieties of sweets, e.g. M&M's, Maltesers, grated chocolate, cut up Mars bars/Snickers bars, nuts, etc. Just go to the chocolate and sweet counter at the supermarket and the world is your oyster!!

Fried Bananas

You can cook maybe 3 bananas at a time in a frying pan. If you have more people, you will need to wash the pan between each batch, or the sauce will not work.

1 **banana**

2cm cube **butter**

1 dessertspoon **sugar**

¼ teaspoon **cinnamon**

double cream, crème fraîche, yogurt, or ice cream to serve

£0.80 /PERSON

2

1

PREP 5 MINS

V

1. Slice the banana in half, lengthways, and then cut each piece in half.

2. Melt the butter in the frying pan, add the sugar and cinnamon. Cook for 1 minute on medium heat. The mixture should be bubbling a little.

3. Add the bananas to the pan and cook for a further minute on a medium heat. The butter and sugar should form a fudgy sauce.

4. Arrange the banana on a plate. Pour the sauce over the banana and add a good serving of cream, crème fraîche, yogurt or ice cream. You can get Greek yogurt with honey which works very well with the bananas.

Squidgy Chocolate Pudding

You can serve it with cream, ice cream, crème fraîche or custard! It should have a crisp outside and a runny inside and is best served hot.

½ x 250g block of **butter**

¾ mug soft **brown sugar**

4 **eggs**, beaten

200g block of **dark cooking chocolate**

1 teaspoon **vanilla extract**

½ mug **self-raising flour**

1. Preheat the oven to 180°C fan oven/200°C/Gas 6. Grease a dish, it should be about 18cm x 23cm and approximately 5cm deep. If you don't have one, use your casserole dish.

2. Mix the butter and sugar together and beat well with a wooden spoon. Add the eggs and beat well.

3. Melt the chocolate gently in a bowl over a pan of simmering water.

4. Once it is all melted, add to the sugar, butter and egg mixture along with the vanilla extract. Mix well.

5. Add the flour and stir in with a metal spoon. Pour into the greased dish and cook for 20-25 minutes. The outside will be crisp and the inside runny.

Boozy Chocolate Trifle

Raspberries are the best fruit to use, but you could also use apricots or pineapple. You will need to chop larger fruits up a little.

1 **chocolate Swiss roll**

¼ mug **sherry**, brandy, Tia Maria or Cointreau

300g tin **raspberries**

300ml tub of **double cream**

2 tablespoons **sugar**

1 **Cadbury's Flake**

1. Slice the Swiss roll into 2.5cm pieces and arrange around the bottom of a dish. A glass dish is preferable, but a casserole dish will work just as well.

2. Pour the liquor evenly over the cake.

3. Put the raspberries and ½ the juice from the tin over the cake.

4. Whip the cream and sugar with a whisk until thickened and spread over the top.

5. Decorate the top with the broken-up flake. Leave in the fridge for 2-3 hours until set.

Menu 1

Monday   Lamb Cobbler p57

Tuesday   rest of Lamb Cobbler

Wednesday   Chicken Hot Pot p75

Thursday   eat rest of Chicken Hot Pot

Friday   Bacon and Potato Bake p120

Saturday   rest of Bacon and Potato Bake

Sunday   Salsa Salad to share p47

check cupboards for:

- mixed herbs
- tomato purée
- freeze-dried basil
- self-raising flour
- stock cubes
- garlic
- Worcestershire sauce
- olive oil

Shopping List

- bread
- cereal
- milk
- butter
- spread
- sandwich fillings
- 3 onions
- 3 carrots
- 6 medium potatoes
- celery (use any spare to eat with sandwiches)
- 6 tomatoes
- 1 curly leaf lettuce
- 1 lemon
- 3 spring onions
- 6 eggs (use spare for sandwiches)
- 250g Cheddar cheese
- suet
- 250g lamb mince
- 4 chicken thighs
- 10 rashers streaky bacon
- 300ml pot of double cream
- 400g tin chopped tomatoes

> Here you are cooking 4 times and sharing Sunday lunch. Again, assuming that you will have cereal for breakfast and sandwiches for lunch, the cost will be approximately £16-18.

Shopping List

- bread
- milk
- cereal
- sandwich fillings
- 7 potatoes
- 2 onions
- small bunch of spring
  onions
- 4 mushrooms
- red pepper
- salad for burgers
- 2 large sausages (buy a
  pack and put the rest
  in the freezer)
- 1 small chicken breast
- 250g pack beef mince
- 125g pack lamb mince
- 150g pack ready-to-
  wok noodles
- 6 eggs
- 250g pack
  Cheddar cheese
- tin baked beans
- 185g tin tuna
- 2 flat burger buns
- 2 small pieces frozen
  cod or haddock

Menu 2

Monday	Spicy Risotto p62
Tuesday	Fisherman's Pie p93
Wednesday	rest of Fisherman's Pie
Thursday	Sausage Soup p55
Friday	rest of Sausage Soup
Saturday	Beefburgers - to share p130
Sunday	Chicken Noodles p148

check cupboards for:

- oil
- rice
- pilav rice
  seasoning
- curry paste
- freeze-dried
  coriander
- butter
- pasta
- freeze-dried
  parsley
- soy sauce
- freeze-dried
  chives
- stock cubes
- Worcestershire
  sauce
- garlic

Here you are being quite generous and cooking 5 times and sharing twice.
Costs only between £14 - 16 for the week. This includes stuff for
breakfast and sandwiches for lunch.

Menu 3

Monday	Chorizo Couscous p65
Tuesday	eat rest of cold Chorizo Couscous
Wednesday	Italian Soup p53
Thursday	eat rest of Italian Soup
Friday	Chicken Hot Pot p75
Saturday	eat rest of Chicken Hot Pot
Sunday	Tuna Hash p66

check cupboards for:
- veg and chicken stock cubes
- garlic
- Worcestershire sauce
- butter
- tomato purée
- basil
- couscous

Shopping List

- 4 carrots
- 6 potatoes
- celery
- 3 medium onions
- 1 red onion
- 1 red pepper
- 2 tomatoes
- small packet macaroni
- 1 can chickpeas
- 2 small chorizo sausages
- 4 chicken thighs
- 400g tin tomatoes
- 185g tin tuna
- 340g tin tomatoes
- frozen spinach
- bread
- milk
- cereal
- sandwich fillings

This one is for when you are really broke and should cost approximately £14-16 for the week.

Shopping List

- 1 onion
- 5 potatoes
- small piece of cucumber
- 1 fat red chilli
- 5 mushrooms
- 150g green beans
- 1 lemon
- 1 courgette
- salad for Fri, Sat, Sun
- 6 eggs + 3 spare
  for sandwiches
- 200g block Feta
  cheese
- 1 kg minced beef
- 250g minced beef
- 8 slices streaky bacon
- small carton crème
  fraîche
- sun-dried tomatoes
- small tin sweetcorn
- 400g tin tomatoes
- 250g pack of
  cooked mackerel
- bread
- milk
- cereal
- sandwich fillings
- butter/spread

Menu 4

Monday Spag Bol p63

Tuesday Rest of Spag Bol

Wednesday Smoked Mackerel Pasta salad p50

Thursday Rest of cold Smoked Mackerel salad

Friday Corn Fritters, leave 1/2 the mix uncooked in the fridge p68

Saturday Rest of the Corn Fritters and Chilli Sauce

Sunday Mum and Dad visit Meatloaf with Baked Potatoes p129

check cupboards for:

- basil
- olive oil
- wholegrain
  mustard
- wine vinegar
- pasta
- garlic
- tomato purée
- beef stock
  cube
- mixed herbs
- flour
- cornflour
- spaghetti

Mum and Dad around on Sunday, but this week will still only cost approximately £18-20.

index

thanks...

This book would not have been possible without the help of many people. My husband Ron and my sons, Ben and Tim, have worked tirelessly to help me.

Thanks again to my very good friends, Fran, for her wonderful proofreading and to Cathryn, for her help in the kitchen.

Many others came to collect and eat food on our photography days. Without them, much food would have been wasted, which is never a good thing!

Thanks to Tim and Ben's friends who have allowed us to use their faces for the front cover. Your free copy is on it's way!

Josh Smith, Katy Bosanko, Josh Feben, Daniella Clements, Deb Smith, Andy Tiffen, Tommy Andrewartha, Phil Hatton, Felix Page, Jo Skinner, Joel Bennett, Michael Pearce, Rav Hayer, Patrick Wilson, Kat Thomas, Jan Moys, Calum Maciver, Rachel Tiffen, Marianne Matthews, Emma Page, Michelle Crispin, Gareth Matthews, Payin Swazey Attafuah, Mary-Jane Attafuah, Chester See, Ems Smith, Jon Herring, Charlie Gregson, Nathanael Bennett, Paul Cannon, James Malbon, Jess Whitbread, Tom Whitbread, Tim Crispin, Naomi Badu, Rach Clements, Hannah Clements, Naomi Clements, Nathaniel Ledwidge, Tekiva Ledwidge, Peter Kent, Beccy Catley, Matt Bentley, Nicola Goodwin, Leanne Clack, Trudy Willoughby, Cerys Duffty, Amy Banham-Hall, Jonathan Ingham, Tom Povey, Nicole May, Emily Malbon, Ross Macfarlane, Amy Macfarlane, Kirsty Macfarlane, Richard Wells, Juliet Adekambi, Simon William Burns, Sharon Makinde, Rachel Donley, Hannah Rich, Nathan Clements, Rachel Phillipps, Odele Caldecourt, Ben McCalla, Dan Richter, Jon Povey, Peter Goult, Connie Haywood, Jez Hill, Ed Gent, Jenny Copperwheat, Dan Copperwheat, Clarence Bissessar, Sarju Patel, Chris Low, Gabbie D'Mello, Esther Gore, Polly West, Kerry Cannon, Kirsty Crooks, Gareth Paton, Lizzie De Kraan, Jonathan Cannon, Matt Skinner, Luke Clements, Lizzie Fieldsend, Leland Fieldsend and Paul Summerville

Acknowledgements to Daniel Midgley (goodreasonblog.blogspot.com) for the free font we have used in the menus. Love it.

© 2010 Joy May

All rights reserved. No part of this book may be reproduced, stored in a retrieval system, or transmitted, in any form or by any means, electronic, mechanical, photocopying, recording or otherwise without the prior permission of the author.

Published by: Intrade (GB) Ltd

contact: joymay@mac.com

Author: Joy May

Printed in China

1st Edition: 2002
Revised Edition: 2006
2nd Edition: March 2011
First print of 2nd Edition: March 2011
ISBN: 9780954317997
ISBN: 0-9543179-9-8

Photography and design: Tim May at www.milkbottlephotography.co.uk

Design: Ben May at www.milkbottledesigns.co.uk

Proofreading: Fran Maciver

Editor: Ron May